EVERY BELIEVER'S GUIDE TO PROPHECY

HEARING GOD'S VOICE AND SPEAKING HIS HEART

TOM CORNELL

EVERY BELIEVER'S GUIDE TO PROPHECY
HEARING GOD'S VOICE AND SPEAKING HIS HEART

TOM CORNELL

Copyright © 2025 by Tom Cornell

All rights reserved.

No portion of this book may be reproduced in any form or by any means without written permission from the publisher or author, except as permitted by U.S. copyright law. First edition.

Paperback ISBN: 979-8-9925380-9-0

Bible quotations are taken from:

The New King James Version® (NKJV). Copyright © 1982 by Thomas Nelson. Used by permission. All rights reserved.

The Holy Bible, New International Version®, NIV®. Copyright © 1973, 1978, 1984, 2011 by Biblica, Inc. Used with permission of Zondervan. All rights reserved worldwide. www.zondervan.com

The ESV® Bible (The Holy Bible, English Standard Version®), © 2001 by Crossway, a publishing ministry of Good News Publishers. Used by permission. All rights reserved."

CONTENTS

Introduction	vii
1. Understanding the Prophetic Gift	1
2. Hearing God's Voice	14
3. Developing Prophetic Sensitivity	28
4. Prophecy and the Word of God	41
5. The Heart of Prophecy	48
6. How to Deliver a Prophetic Word	55
7. Testing and Judging Prophetic Words	63
8. Common Pitfalls in the Prophetic	69
9. Prophetic Protocol in the Local Church	74
10. Growing in Prophetic Boldness	82
11. Activating the Gift of Prophecy	88
12. Prophetic Lifestyle	101
13. The Future of Prophetic Ministry	107
Conclusion	113
About the Author	117

INTRODUCTION
WHY PROPHECY IS FOR EVERY BELIEVER

When you hear the word "prophecy," what comes to mind? For many, it conjures up images of extraordinary visions, cryptic messages, or people with seemingly otherworldly experiences—what some might call "third heaven" moments. Prophecy often feels distant, mystical, and unattainable, reserved for a select few who are uniquely gifted or spiritually elite.

But what if I told you prophecy was never meant to be out of reach? What if it wasn't as complicated as we've made it? My experience has been that most people feel intimidated by the very idea of being prophetic, thinking they don't have what it takes to hear from God. Yet, the truth is refreshingly simple: as believers, we are sheep, and Jesus, the Good Shepherd, said His sheep hear His voice (John 10:27).

Think about that for a moment. Hearing God's voice is not a reward for the spiritually advanced; it's the birthright of every believer. Prophecy, at its core, is hearing God's voice and speaking His heart. It's less about dramatic encounters and more about a relationship rooted in love and trust. It's not reserved for the "prophets" in the church but available to anyone who follows Jesus.

The Bible describes prophecy as a gift designed for edification, exhortation, and comfort (1 Corinthians 14:3). In other words, it's not about predicting the future or impressing others with spiritual insight. It's about building people up, encouraging them, and pointing them to the heart of God.

Prophecy is one of the most practical and powerful ways we can partner with God to bring His kingdom to earth. In this book, we'll explore what it means to embrace the prophetic as an everyday part of your life. We'll dismantle the myths that make prophecy feel intimidating or exclusive, and we'll dive into the practical steps you can take to grow in hearing God's voice.

Whether you're brand new to the prophetic or looking to deepen your understanding, my hope is that you'll come away feeling empowered to step into this beautiful gift with confidence and joy. Prophecy is not about having all the answers or achieving perfection. It's about listening to the heart of the Father and letting His love flow through you to others.

It's about being willing to say, "Speak, Lord, for Your servant is listening" (1 Samuel 3:10). So let's set aside the mysticism and intimidation, and discover together how simple, beautiful, and life-changing the prophetic can be. Let's begin this journey of hearing God's voice and speaking His heart.

CHAPTER 1
UNDERSTANDING THE PROPHETIC GIFT

Prophecy is one of the most misunderstood spiritual gifts in the body of Christ. Many people believe that prophecy is reserved for an elite group of individuals—those who hold the office of a prophet. However, the New Testament clearly teaches that the gift of prophecy is available to every believer. In 1 Corinthians 14:1, Paul encourages believers to:

> *"pursue love and eagerly desire spiritual gifts, especially that you may prophesy."* NIV

This instruction wasn't directed to a select few but to the entire church. Prophecy, at its core, is simply hearing God's heart and speaking what He says. It's a way for believers to encourage, strengthen, and comfort others through the inspiration of the Holy Spirit. Understanding the prophetic gift begins with knowing its purpose, biblical foundations, and how it operates.

The Office of a Prophet vs. the Gift of Prophecy

One of the first distinctions to understand in the realm of the prophetic is the difference between the office of a prophet and the gift of prophecy. The office of a prophet is a specific calling within the fivefold ministry, as outlined in Ephesians 4:11, where Paul states that God gave some to be apostles, prophets, evangelists, pastors, and teachers.

Those called to the office of a prophet are equipped to provide spiritual direction, correction, and insight into God's purposes for individuals, groups, nations, or even the church at large. Prophets often carry a unique burden to intercede and speak on behalf of God in ways that bring alignment and clarity to His purposes. Their role is foundational to equipping the saints and building the church, and not everyone is called to this office.

The gift of prophecy, on the other hand, is a spiritual gift made available to any believer through the Holy Spirit (1 Corinthians 12:10). While prophets operate with a higher level of authority and responsibility, the gift of prophecy is intended for every believer to use in a way that strengthens, encourages, and comforts others (1 Corinthians 14:3).

This gift is not limited by age, spiritual maturity, or position in the church; rather, it is an expression of God's love and an invitation for all believers to participate in revealing His heart to those around them. While the office of a prophet carries the weight of leadership and broader influence, the gift of prophecy is personal and relational, allowing any believer to minister to others in everyday life.

Paul makes it clear that while not everyone will hold the office of a prophet, every believer can and should eagerly desire the gift of prophecy (1 Corinthians 14:1). This distinction helps to prevent confusion or feelings of inadequacy among believers. Just because someone does not operate as a prophet does not mean they cannot hear from God and share His words.

In fact, Paul emphasizes the importance of prophecy for building up the church, making it one of the most accessible and practical gifts for fostering unity and spiritual growth within the body of Christ (1 Corinthians 14:3-4). Understanding the difference between the office of a prophet and the gift of prophecy ensures that believers operate within their God-given roles without overstepping boundaries or undervaluing their potential.

It also creates a culture of honor in the church, where the prophetic office is respected, and the prophetic gift is encouraged. Recognizing this distinction allows believers to embrace their role in the prophetic while remaining teachable and submitted to godly leadership. In this way, the body of Christ can function in harmony, with both prophets and prophetic believers working together to reveal God's heart to the world.

The Purpose of Prophecy

Prophecy has always been a vital aspect of God's relationship with His people, serving as a conduit for Him to communicate *His heart, will, and Intent*. In the New Testament, prophecy takes on a distinct role compared to its Old Testament counterpart. While Old Testament prophecy often involved warnings, judgment, and declarations of God's sovereignty, *New Testament* prophecy focuses on revealing *His love, grace, and redemptive purposes.*

This shift aligns with the covenant of grace established through Jesus Christ, emphasizing how God desires to build

His church and edify His people through words of encouragement and hope. The primary purposes of New Testament prophecy are outlined in 1 Corinthians 14:3:

- **Edification**
- **Exhortation**
- **Comfort**

Edification involves building others up in their faith, strengthening their confidence in God, and encouraging spiritual growth. Prophecy also *exhorts* believers, urging them to press on in their walk with God and remain steadfast despite challenges. Finally, prophecy brings *comfort*, offering peace, hope, and reassurance to those facing trials or uncertainties.

These three purposes demonstrate that prophecy is not about condemnation or instilling fear but about helping believers connect with God's love and truth in a personal and transformative way. Prophecy also serves as a powerful tool for unity within the body of Christ. When believers share prophetic words, they often bring clarity and affirmation to situations that others are experiencing, fostering a sense of connection and mutual encouragement.

This is why Paul emphasizes the importance of prophecy in corporate settings—it builds up the entire church. Prophetic words often confirm what God is already speaking to someone's heart, encouraging them to trust His guidance and take bold steps of faith. This communal aspect of prophecy strengthens relationships and promotes a culture of love and trust within the church.

Ultimately, the purpose of prophecy is to reveal God's heart to His people. Every prophetic word should reflect His character, drawing people closer to Him and pointing them to Jesus. As Revelation 19:10 declares,

"The testimony of Jesus is the spirit of prophecy." NKJV

Whether spoken to an individual or shared in a corporate setting, true prophecy will always glorify God, align with Scripture, and lead to transformation. It is a divine invitation to partner with the Holy Spirit in speaking life, truth, and hope into the lives of others.

How Prophecy Operates in the Life of a Believer

Prophecy is not about predicting the future or demonstrating spiritual prowess; it is about partnering with the Holy Spirit to release God's heart, will, and truth over individuals, situations, and even communities. At its core, *prophecy flows from a deep relationship with God and a desire to see His purposes fulfilled on earth.*

It is not a mystical or unattainable practice but an accessible gift for believers who are willing to listen, step out in faith, and speak with humility. To prophesy is to act as a vessel through which God's words can bring transformation and encouragement. One of the key principles of prophetic ministry is that it operates through the Holy Spirit.

Prophecy is not something conjured by human effort or intuition; it begins with hearing and recognizing the voice of the Spirit. As believers grow in their relationship with the Holy Spirit, they learn to discern His whispers—whether through impressions, visions, scriptures, or spoken words. These revelations are meant to align with the Word of God and reflect His character. The ability to prophesy increases as believers cultivate a lifestyle of prayer, worship, and intimacy with the Lord.

A close relationship with the Spirit ensures that prophetic words remain authentic and Spirit-led, rather than driven by personal opinions or desires. Prophecy also operates by faith. Speaking prophetically often requires stepping out with a willingness to risk being wrong or misunderstood. This is especially true because, as Paul explains in 1 Corinthians 13:9,

> *"we see in part and prophesy in part."* NKJV

No prophetic word is delivered with perfect clarity, but faith enables believers to trust God's leading even when they have only a glimpse of what He is revealing. Faith stretches believers to act on the prompting of the Holy Spirit and trust that He will use their obedience to impact others. As believers practice prophetic ministry, their confidence grows, not in themselves but in God's faithfulness to speak through them.

Another essential component of prophecy is humility. Those who prophesy must remember that they are simply vessels, not the source of the message. Humility acknowledges that all prophetic insight comes from God and must be handled with care, ensuring that words are delivered in love and submission to spiritual authority.

This mindset protects believers from pride or the temptation to misuse prophetic gifts for personal gain. It also fosters accountability, as prophetic words are tested against Scripture and the discernment of mature leaders. Humility keeps prophecy centered on serving others and glorifying God, rather than elevating the individual delivering the message.

Biblical Foundations of Prophecy

Understanding how prophecy operates in the life of a believer begins with its biblical foundation. Throughout Scripture, prophecy is presented as a means through which God communicates with His people. In Joel 2:28-29, God declares,

> "I will pour out my Spirit on all people. Your sons and daughters will prophesy..." NIV

This Old Testament prophecy is fulfilled in Acts 2 during Pentecost, marking the beginning of a new covenant era where prophecy becomes accessible to all believers. Unlike the Old Testament, where the Spirit rested on select individuals, the New Testament invites all Spirit-filled believers to participate in prophetic ministry. Paul emphasizes this shift in 1 Corinthians 14:1, encouraging the church to,

> "eagerly desire spiritual gifts, especially that you may prophesy." NIV

This verse highlights prophecy as a normal and encouraged part of the Christian life. Paul's instruction reflects the importance of prophecy for building up the body of Christ. It is not a gift reserved for the spiritually elite but one that every believer should desire and pursue.

Prophecy's accessibility to all demonstrates God's desire for His people to share in His work of encouragement, exhortation, and comfort. As stated before Revelation 19:10, is key which states,

> "The testimony of Jesus is the spirit of prophecy." NKJV

This verse underscores the Christ-centered nature of prophetic ministry. True prophecy always points back to Jesus, revealing His heart and advancing His purposes. Whether delivered through a personal word or a corporate message, prophecy that aligns with Jesus' testimony will reflect His love, grace, and truth.

This Christ-centered focus safeguards believers from straying into self-promotion or manipulation, ensuring that prophecy remains an extension of God's character and mission. By rooting prophetic ministry in these biblical principles, believers can approach prophecy with confidence and clarity.

Prophecy is not a mysterious or unapproachable gift but a tangible expression of God's desire to communicate with His people. When believers understand how prophecy operates through the Holy Spirit, by faith, and with humility—and when they recognize its scriptural foundations—they can step into this gift as active participants in revealing God's heart to the world.

Why Prophecy is Important for Every Believer

Prophecy is not just a spiritual gift for a select few; it is a vital tool for every believer to use in building God's kingdom. The ability to hear God's voice and speak His words is an extraordinary privilege and a responsibility that strengthens both individual believers and the corporate church.

While prophecy can seem intimidating or out of reach for some, Scripture encourages all believers to eagerly desire this gift (1 Corinthians 14:1) because of its far-reaching impact. Understanding the importance of prophecy helps believers see how they can contribute to God's work on earth by releasing His love, truth, and encouragement.

One of the most significant reasons prophecy is important is that it helps build the church. Prophecy is uniquely designed to strengthen the faith of believers, unify the body of Christ, and create an atmosphere of encouragement and growth. Paul emphasizes in 1 Corinthians 14:3-4 that prophecy is meant to edify, exhort, and comfort believers.

By speaking God's words, prophecy fortifies individuals who may be struggling, giving them clarity, hope, and direction. When this happens on a larger scale in a church setting, it fosters unity, as people see God's Spirit moving in tangible ways. Prophecy has the power to affirm God's plans, confirm decisions, and ignite a passion for collective obedience to His will.

In this way, prophecy is a gift not only for individuals but for the entire church community. Another reason prophecy is vital is that it connects believers to God's heart. When someone prophesies, they are not simply sharing their thoughts or opinions; they are communicating what God desires to reveal. This requires the believer to be in a posture of listening to the Holy Spirit and discerning His voice.

The process of receiving and delivering a prophetic word draws believers into deeper intimacy with God. They learn to recognize His voice, trust His leading, and depend on His wisdom. This connection is transformative, as it shifts believers from simply knowing about God to walking closely with Him in a dynamic relationship. Each prophetic experience reinforces the reality that God is actively involved in their lives and that He desires to speak through them to impact others.

Prophecy is also important because it demonstrates God's love in a deeply personal way. One of the most beautiful aspects of prophecy is its ability to reveal that God sees, knows, and cares for each individual. A prophetic word can penetrate the hardest hearts and bring reassurance to those who feel unseen or forgotten. For example, when someone receives a prophetic message that speaks directly to their current situation, it becomes undeniable evidence that God is aware of their struggles and has a plan for their future.

This personal connection to God's love often leads to healing, restoration, and renewed faith. It also creates an opportunity for the church to become a place where people encounter God's love in a tangible and meaningful way. Moreover, prophecy is a powerful tool for advancing God's kingdom because it brings heaven's perspective to earthly situations.

When believers prophesy, they align themselves with God's vision for individuals, communities, and even nations. This alignment allows them to release words of hope and transformation that inspire others to step into God's purposes. Prophecy often serves as a catalyst for action, encouraging people to obey God's call, step out in faith, and trust Him for the impossible.

Whether it's calling someone into their God-given destiny or speaking peace into a chaotic situation, prophecy has the unique ability to shift circumstances and reveal God's power at work. Finally, prophecy equips believers to partner with God in His mission. By learning to hear His voice and speak His words, believers become active participants in His plan to bring redemption and restoration to the world. Prophecy is not about showing off spiritual gifts or gaining recognition—it's about serving others and glorifying God.

As believers embrace the importance of prophecy, they discover the joy of being used by the Holy Spirit to bring life, encouragement, and transformation to those around them. In doing so, they fulfill their role as ambassadors of Christ, carrying His love and truth wherever they go.

In summary, prophecy is an indispensable gift for every believer. It builds the church, fosters intimacy with God, reveals His love, and empowers believers to partner with Him in bringing His kingdom to earth. When believers understand the value of prophecy and step into this gift with humility and faith, they become conduits of God's heart, making a profound impact on their communities and the world.

Prophecy is a gift available to every believer, designed to edify, encourage, and comfort others through the power of the Holy Spirit. While the office of a prophet is a specific calling within the fivefold ministry, the gift of prophecy is for all believers who are willing to listen to God and speak His words in faith and humility. Prophecy reveals God's love, strengthens the church, and connects believers to His heart in profound ways.

The New Testament highlights that prophecy is not about judgment or fear, as seen in the Old Testament, but about revealing God's love, purposes, and intentions. Through prophecy, believers grow in intimacy with God, demonstrate His care for others, and play an active role in building His kingdom. Prophecy always aligns with Scripture, points to Jesus, and reflects the heart of God.

When believers eagerly desire and operate in this gift, they become vessels of God's voice, bringing clarity, direction, and hope to individuals and communities. The practice of prophecy is not about perfection but faith and obedience, trusting the Holy Spirit to guide and use them.

Activations

1. **Ask the Holy Spirit to Speak:** Find a quiet moment to pray and ask God to reveal His thoughts for someone. Be still and attentive to impressions, words, scriptures, or images He may give you.
2. **Write Down What You Sense:** Without overthinking, write down or record anything that comes to your mind. Remember, prophecy often comes in part (1 Corinthians 13:9), so trust what you receive.
3. **Speak with Faith and Humility:** Share what you feel led to say with the person God puts on your heart. Use phrases like, "I feel like God might be saying..." or "Does this resonate with you?" This invites confirmation and dialogue without pressure.
4. **Test the Prophetic Word:** Ensure the word aligns with Scripture and reflects God's love, encouragement, and truth. Avoid personal bias or assumptions.
5. **Practice Regularly:** Prophecy grows as you use it. Find safe spaces—such as small groups, prayer meetings, or trusted friends—where you can step out in faith and learn to hear God's voice more clearly. By activating the prophetic gift in your life, you open the door for God to work through you to bless others and build His church. Step out in faith, and watch how God uses you to bring His love and truth to the world around you.

CHAPTER 2
HEARING GOD'S VOICE

One of the greatest privileges of being a believer is learning to hear the voice of God. It's an incredible reality that the Creator of the universe desires to have a personal relationship with His children and actively speaks to them. Jesus affirmed this truth in John 10:27, saying,

"My sheep listen to my voice; I know them, and they follow me." NIV

This verse not only highlights the importance of hearing God's voice but also reveals the intimacy and trust that comes with following Him. Hearing God's voice is not reserved for a select few or an elite group of super-spiritual Christians. It is a gift and a promise available to every believer who has a relationship with Him.

It's not about striving, earning, or achieving a certain level of spiritual maturity. Instead, it's about being open, willing, and intentional in cultivating a connection with God. The process of hearing His voice is a journey—a dynamic and ongoing interaction that grows and deepens over time. It's a relationship, not a formula, and it looks slightly different for each individual because God speaks in ways that are uniquely tailored to how He created us.

In this chapter, we will explore the various ways God speaks to His people, how to discern His voice amidst the noise of life, and how to develop the kind of intimacy with Him that allows His words to resonate clearly in our hearts. Recognizing God's voice begins with understanding His character and His deep desire to guide and communicate with us.

How God Speaks

God speaks in many ways, and His methods are as diverse as the individuals He communicates with. Understanding these ways will help you remain open, attentive, and expectant as you listen for His voice. Every believer has the ability to hear from God because He longs for a close relationship with us. As we examine the different ways He speaks, you may begin to notice how God has already been communicating with you, perhaps in ways you didn't fully recognize before.

The ways God speaks are not limited to a single method or experience. Instead, they are deeply personal and often reflect the unique ways He designed us to connect with Him. The following sections will help you identify these methods, so you can be more sensitive to His leading and better equipped to hear His voice.

Dreams and Visions

Dreams and visions are powerful ways God communicates with His people, offering insight, encouragement, or guidance. Throughout Scripture, we see numerous examples of God speaking in this way. For instance, Joseph interpreted Pharaoh's dreams, revealing a divine plan to prepare for a coming famine (Genesis 41). Similarly, Peter had a vision of unclean animals, which symbolized God's invitation to extend the gospel to the Gentiles (Acts 10).

John's vision on the island of Patmos provided the church with profound revelations about Christ's return and the end times (Revelation). These examples highlight the spiritual significance of dreams and visions in the lives of believers. When God uses dreams and visions, they often contain symbolic meanings that require discernment and prayer to understand.

Unlike straightforward communication, these experiences can feel mysterious or even puzzling at first. For instance, the imagery in a dream might represent a deeper spiritual truth or a specific action God is calling you to take. This is why it is important to approach such experiences with humility and a willingness to seek God's interpretation. As Daniel said in Daniel 2:28,

"There is a God in heaven who reveals mysteries." NIV

If you have a dream or vision that feels spiritually significant, it's helpful to write it down as soon as possible. Documenting the details will allow you to revisit them with clarity and prayerfully seek God's guidance over time. Journaling also helps you notice patterns or recurring themes that may reveal what God is saying to you.

Consulting Scripture is another critical step, as God's Word provides a foundation for interpreting dreams and visions. His messages will always align with His written Word and reflect His character. It's also wise to share your experience with spiritually mature believers who can pray with you and offer insights.

God often confirms His messages through the counsel of others in the body of Christ. Remember, dreams and visions are just one way God communicates. While they can be profound and impactful, they should lead you to greater intimacy with Him, pointing you toward His heart and His purposes.

Impressions and Inner Nudges

God often speaks to His people through subtle impressions or inner nudges, communicating in ways that resonate deeply with our spirits. These impressions can feel like a sudden thought, idea, or unexplainable sense that urges you toward a particular action or awareness.

Unlike an audible voice or dramatic vision, these moments are often quiet, requiring attentiveness and sensitivity to the Holy Spirit. For example, you might feel prompted to pray for someone, encourage them with a specific word, or make a decision you hadn't initially considered. Recognizing these impressions is a vital part of growing in your ability to hear God's voice.

The Bible highlights how God often communicates in a "still, small voice" (1 Kings 19:12). This account of Elijah reminds us that God's voice is not always found in the dramatic or the loud but in the gentle and subtle. Paying attention to these inner nudges requires cultivating spiritual discernment and quieting the noise of our daily lives.

Often, these impressions bring peace, clarity, or a sense of urgency to act, confirming they are from God. Over time, as you practice responding to these inner nudges, you'll grow more confident in distinguishing His voice from your own thoughts or emotions. A practical way to recognize impressions from God is by testing them against Scripture.

God's guidance will always align with His Word and reflect His character. For example, an impression to encourage someone with a specific Scripture or an act of kindness will naturally align with His heart for love and edification. It's also helpful to journal these moments and reflect on the outcomes.

As you document the times you've acted on inner nudges, you may notice patterns that reveal God's faithfulness and guidance. It's important to step out in faith when you sense an impression from God. Even if you're unsure at first, taking a small step of obedience can open the door for greater clarity and confirmation.

For example, sending a message to someone God places on your heart could result in a meaningful conversation or encouragement at just the right time. As you respond to these inner nudges, your sensitivity to the Holy Spirit will increase, deepening your intimacy with God and your ability to hear His voice more clearly.

Scripture

The Bible is the most reliable and consistent way God speaks to His people. As His inspired Word (2 Timothy 3:16), it serves as the foundation for understanding His will and character. Scripture is timeless, offering guidance, correction, and encouragement to believers in every generation. When you open the Bible, you're not just reading ancient texts—you're engaging with God's living and active Word (Hebrews 4:12).

Every verse has the potential to reveal His heart and provide direction for your life.

One way God speaks through Scripture is by illuminating specific verses or passages as you read. You might notice a particular verse standing out, almost as if it were written just for you in that moment. This is often the Holy Spirit highlighting a truth that applies directly to your current situation. For example, a passage about God's faithfulness may resonate when you're facing uncertainty, offering reassurance and strengthening your faith.

These moments are significant because they demonstrate how personal and intimate God's communication is through His Word. Studying Scripture also equips you to recognize God's voice in other forms of communication. Because the Bible reveals His character and ways, it becomes the standard against which all impressions, dreams, or prophetic words are measured.

If what you sense aligns with Scripture, you can trust it as God's voice. However, if something contradicts the Bible, it should be rejected. This is why immersing yourself in Scripture is essential—it grounds you in truth and sharpens your discernment. Meditating on God's Word allows it to take root in your heart, making it easier to hear His voice throughout your day.

As you memorize and reflect on Scripture, the Holy Spirit can bring specific verses to your mind at just the right time. For example, He may remind you of Philippians 4:6-7 when you're feeling anxious, or Psalm 23 when you need reassurance of His presence. These moments show that the Bible is not just a book but a living conversation between God and His people. By engaging with Scripture regularly, you create space for God to speak and guide you in profound and practical ways.

Other People

One of the ways God speaks to us is through other people. As members of the body of Christ, we are called to encourage, teach, and sharpen one another (Ephesians 4:11-12). This can happen in various forms—whether through a sermon, a word of encouragement, or a prophetic insight shared by a fellow believer. These moments of divine communication often come unexpectedly but can bring clarity and direction in ways we may not have anticipated.

God may also use fellow believers to confirm or amplify something He has already spoken to you. For example, you might feel a stirring in your heart about a particular decision, and then, in conversation with a trusted friend, they might share a word that resonates deeply with your spirit. This confirmation can bring peace and assurance, helping you recognize that God is indeed speaking to you.

Being part of a community of faith makes you more attuned to hearing God through the wisdom and counsel of others. However, it's important to stay discerning when receiving words from others. Not everything shared is from God, so it's essential to weigh what's spoken with Scripture and prayer.

The Holy Spirit helps you discern what is true, and when you're connected to a community of believers, you can rely on mutual accountability and support to ensure you're hearing God clearly. Ultimately, God's voice through others is a precious gift, designed to build you up and guide you toward His purposes.

Recognizing the Voice of God vs. Your Own Thoughts

Distinguishing God's voice from your own thoughts or external influences is a skill that develops over time and through experience. While it may be challenging at first, with patience and practice, you will begin to recognize His voice more clearly. Below are some key ways to discern the difference between God's voice, your own thoughts, and other voices that may be present in your life:

1. **God's Voice Aligns with Scripture**

One of the clearest ways to recognize God's voice is to test it against the Word of God. God will never speak in a way that contradicts His written Word, for He is the same yesterday, today, and forever (Hebrews 13:8). If what you sense in your heart doesn't align with the principles found in Scripture, it's likely not from God.

For instance, if you feel prompted to act in a way that fosters division, jealousy, or sin, it's not from God, as His Word consistently calls believers to unity, peace, and holiness (Romans 12:10, Ephesians 4:3). Always measure what you hear against the truth of the Bible, as Scripture serves as a safeguard to ensure that the voice you hear is truly God's.

2. **God's Voice Brings Peace**

Another key characteristic of God's voice is that it brings peace, even in the midst of challenging circumstances. While God may call you to step out in faith or bring a word of correction, His voice will always be accompanied by a deep sense of peace, calm, and clarity. This peace isn't the absence of discomfort or challenge, but a deep inner assurance that comes from knowing you are hearing from God and walking in His will (Colossians 3:15).

On the other hand, when you hear thoughts that are filled with anxiety, fear, or condemnation, these are not from God. Scripture reminds us that God has not given us a spirit of fear but of power, love, and self-control (2 Timothy 1:7). Therefore, if the voice you hear causes you to feel afraid or condemned, it is not from God.

3. God's Voice Is Persistent but Gentle

God speaks to us with persistence, but unlike external pressures or negative influences, He does so gently. His voice doesn't shout or force itself upon us but is tender and inviting. This is different from the voice of the enemy or the world, which often comes with accusations, guilt, or pressure to act quickly and impulsively.

God invites us to listen to His voice and follow Him willingly, without force. He doesn't manipulate or coerce us but draws us near with His love and gentleness (Matthew 11:28-30). When you hear a voice that seems to push you, confuse you, or make you feel like you have no choice, this is likely not God. His voice will always be gentle, like a shepherd calling His sheep to follow (John 10:27).

4. Practice and Experience

Recognizing God's voice is a skill that grows with practice and experience. Just like learning to recognize a friend's voice in a crowd, the more time you spend with God, the more familiar you will become with His voice. When you hear a prompting, try writing it down and reflect on it. Keep a journal of what you believe God is saying and note how it aligns with Scripture and the peace it brings.

Over time, you will be able to look back and see how God has spoken to you in the past and how He has confirmed His voice through circumstances, other people, or Scripture. This practice builds confidence in hearing God's voice. As you grow in experience, you will find it easier to discern His voice amidst the noise of your thoughts and the world around you. The more you practice listening and obeying, the clearer and more distinct His voice will become.

Cultivating Intimacy with God to Hear Clearly

Hearing God's voice is intricately tied to the depth of your relationship with Him. Just as a close friend's voice becomes unmistakable after spending time together, God's voice becomes clearer the more you cultivate intimacy with Him. The closer you draw near to God, the more clearly you will hear Him speak, for He desires to be known and to communicate with those who earnestly seek Him. Building this relationship involves intentional steps of drawing near to Him daily and being intentional about creating space for His presence. Here are some ways to deepen your relationship with God, allowing you to hear His voice more clearly:

1. Daily Prayer and Worship

One of the most vital practices in cultivating intimacy with God is setting aside intentional time for prayer and worship each day. Prayer is a two-way conversation, not just an opportunity to present your requests and concerns but also a chance to listen for God's guidance and promptings.

When you make prayer a daily habit, you open your heart to hear from God and invite Him to speak into your life. It is in these quiet moments that God often reveals His heart, gives direction, and brings peace. Worship is equally powerful in creating an atmosphere where God's presence becomes tangible.

When you worship, whether through singing, adoration, or simply reflecting on His greatness, you invite the Holy Spirit to come and fill the space, making it easier to hear His voice. Worship also helps align your heart with His, attuning you to His frequency. It silences the distractions and noise of the world, positioning you to receive from Him.

2. Meditation on Scripture

The Bible is God's Word to His people, and meditating on it regularly is essential for cultivating intimacy with Him. When you meditate on Scripture, you invite God's truth to sink deeply into your heart and mind. The Holy Spirit works through Scripture to reveal deeper truths and highlight verses that speak directly to your situation. Meditation isn't just about reading the Bible; it's about reflecting on it, asking God to illuminate it, and waiting for His voice to speak through it.

As you meditate, you may begin to notice that certain passages resonate with you in a fresh way, or that new insights emerge that bring clarity or direction. It's often in these moments of focused reflection that God speaks directly to your spirit, guiding you through His Word and bringing His wisdom into your daily life. The more you make a habit of meditating on Scripture, the more familiar you become with God's voice as He speaks through His Word.

3. Eliminate Distractions

In today's world, distractions are everywhere, making it more difficult to hear the still, small voice of God. Between our phones, social media, work demands, and the constant flow of information, it can feel nearly impossible to create moments of quiet where we can truly hear from God. Yet, the Bible tells us that God often speaks in the stillness, as He did when He spoke to Elijah in 1 Kings 19:11-12.

In order to hear God's voice more clearly, it is important to eliminate distractions that may prevent you from fully focusing on Him. Set aside time each day to be alone with God, free from the noise and busyness of life. This might mean turning off your phone, stepping away from social media, or finding a quiet place where you can be undisturbed.

Silence creates an environment where you can listen attentively for God's voice. The more you prioritize silence and solitude, the more you will cultivate a space in your life where God's voice becomes easier to hear.

4. Obedience to His Voice

One of the most significant ways to deepen your ability to hear God clearly is through obedience to His voice. As you begin to recognize God's voice, it's essential to respond in obedience, even in the small things. Every step of obedience strengthens your relationship with Him and builds trust, making it easier to hear Him in the future.

When you obey what God speaks to you, whether it's a call to pray for someone, step out in faith, or adjust your behavior, you demonstrate your willingness to follow His lead. This act of obedience invites more of His guidance into your life. The more you respond to His voice, the more you will be attuned to hearing Him in the future, as obedience builds the pathway to deeper communication.

Additionally, each act of obedience increases your spiritual sensitivity, allowing you to discern His voice with greater clarity and confidence. By committing to daily prayer, worship, meditation on Scripture, eliminating distractions, and responding in obedience, you cultivate a deeper intimacy with God that makes hearing His voice clearer and more profound.

These practices help you tune your heart to His, allowing you to not only hear His voice but to live in alignment with His will for your life. As you deepen your relationship with God, you will find that His voice becomes more distinct, more powerful, and more relevant to your daily walk with Him. The more you cultivate these habits, the more you will hear and recognize His voice, guiding you in every area of your life.

Activations

1. **Listen Intentionally:** Find a quiet place and ask God to speak to you. Write down any impressions, scriptures, or thoughts that come to mind.
2. **Pray with Scripture:** Choose a passage and ask the Holy Spirit to reveal what He wants to say through it. Reflect on how it applies to your life.
3. **Practice Journaling:** Start a journal where you record your conversations with God. Over time, you'll begin to recognize patterns in how He speaks to you.
4. **Ask for Confirmation:** Share what you feel God is saying with a trusted mentor or friend. They can help confirm and encourage you as you grow in hearing His voice.

Hearing God's voice is a journey, not a destination. As you commit to seeking Him daily, you'll grow in confidence and clarity in recognizing His voice. God is always speaking—are you ready to listen?

CHAPTER 3
DEVELOPING PROPHETIC SENSITIVITY

Prophetic sensitivity is essential for anyone who seeks to walk in the gift of prophecy. It involves more than just speaking words on behalf of God; it's about tuning your heart to hear His promptings and becoming more attuned to the Holy Spirit's subtle leadings. Prophecy flows from a place of intimate connection with God, and sensitivity to His voice is a key component of that relationship.

Prophetic sensitivity requires cultivating the ability to recognize and respond to the voice of God, and it demands an openness to the Holy Spirit's direction in every moment. This chapter will explore how to develop this sensitivity, with a focus on the pivotal role of the Holy Spirit, how to be more responsive to God's nudges, and the critical importance of discernment in distinguishing God's voice from other influences.

Prophecy is not simply about speaking a word but about being in tune with the movement of God in your spirit and being aware of the world around you. The prophetic gift is deeply relational, relying on a continual flow of communication between God and the believer. Just as you would learn to recognize a close friend's voice, so too you must develop a familiarity with God's voice.

The more you respond to His gentle promptings, the more you'll grow in sensitivity and clarity. Prophecy comes alive in a heart that is attuned to God's desires, one that listens actively, responds faithfully, and learns to trust His leading. Developing this level of prophetic sensitivity is not instantaneous but grows with time, practice, and intentional pursuit of deeper intimacy with God.

The Role of the Holy Spirit in Prophecy

The Holy Spirit is the foundational and central figure in the prophetic life. He is not only the source of the prophetic gift, but He also empowers believers to both hear and speak the words of God. Without the Holy Spirit, prophecy would not be a supernatural act of divine communication; instead, it would be nothing more than a natural gift—lacking the profound insight, clarity, and transformative power that make prophecy effective and life-changing.

In the absence of the Holy Spirit, prophecy would be limited to human interpretation, prone to error and lacking the authority and life that come from God alone. The Holy Spirit is the One who stirs up the prophetic gift within us, making us more sensitive to God's heart, thoughts, desires, and plans for others. He speaks directly to our hearts, guiding us to accurately interpret and communicate God's will.

Through the Holy Spirit, we gain the divine ability not just to speak, but to speak with the authority, wisdom, and insight that reflect God's true heart. In 1 Corinthians 12, Paul underscores that prophecy is a gift of the Spirit, distributed according to His will. This means that every prophetic word, every prophetic encounter, is rooted in the Holy Spirit's empowering presence. He is the One who awakens the gift within us and gives us the grace to step into the flow of God's prophetic purpose.

The Holy Spirit does not merely equip us with the ability to speak prophetic words; He works in our hearts and minds to make us more attuned to God's whispers and promptings. The depth of God's heart is revealed through the Holy Spirit, and it is through Him that we gain a deeper understanding of His desires and will for individuals, communities, and the world.

The Holy Spirit's role is not limited to the initiation of prophetic words but extends to our ongoing relationship with Him. He teaches us how to listen to His voice, how to recognize His movements in our spirit, and how to distinguish His voice from the distractions of our own thoughts or external influences. Prophecy is not just about speaking, but also about learning to listen carefully and discern the leading of the Holy Spirit in every moment.

It is through continuous relationship with the Holy Spirit that we develop prophetic sensitivity, where we become more attuned to the ways He communicates—whether through impressions, visions, dreams, or inner peace. This sensitivity grows as we consistently yield to His guidance through prayer, worship, and silence, giving ourselves the space to hear from Him. This dependency on the Holy Spirit is not a one-time experience but a continual process.

We are called to live in constant reliance upon Him, not only for prophetic utterance but for all areas of our spiritual lives. The more we yield to the Holy Spirit's guidance, the more we become open and responsive to His leadings. However, this requires that we cultivate an intimate relationship with Him. The Holy Spirit works best in a heart that is soft, open, and actively seeking His direction.

In this environment of intimacy, God can speak freely and we can discern His voice more clearly. Without a heart that is open to His promptings, we risk becoming dull to His voice, making it more challenging to discern what He is saying. Furthermore, as we learn to recognize the voice of the Holy Spirit, we gain the ability to differentiate between what is from God and what is from other sources—be it our own desires, the enemy's lies, or even well-meaning advice from others.

It is only through the Holy Spirit's empowerment that we can filter through these competing voices and arrive at an accurate, prophetic understanding. The deeper our intimacy with the Holy Spirit, the more sharply we can distinguish between His voice and others, enabling us to walk with greater prophetic clarity.

The Holy Spirit is not just about giving us words to speak but about teaching us to discern His presence, to recognize His guidance in each moment, and to remain sensitive to His heart and will. Thus, prophetic sensitivity is a continual process of yielding, learning, and growing in our relationship with the Holy Spirit. It requires humility and a willingness to be led by Him, trusting that He will guide us into truth and will empower us to speak words of life, wisdom, and love.

As we learn to listen closely and respond faithfully to His voice, the prophetic gift becomes more than just a momentary word—it becomes a way of life, rooted in deep dependence on the Holy Spirit, marked by an ever-increasing sensitivity to His promptings. Through this ongoing process of learning to hear, discern, and respond to the Holy Spirit, we grow into more faithful and effective vessels of prophecy, used to reveal God's heart and bring transformation to the world around us.

Become More Sensitive to God's Promptings

Becoming more sensitive to God's promptings is not something that happens overnight—it requires intentionality, practice, and a heart that seeks to deepen its connection with God. The key to developing prophetic sensitivity is cultivating a lifestyle of intimacy with God, where His voice becomes the most important influence in your life. This intimacy isn't just about seeking God for prophetic words but about creating a relationship where His presence is the center of all you do.

The more time you spend with God, the more attuned your heart becomes to His voice, and the more easily you'll recognize His promptings. One of the most effective ways to become more sensitive to God's voice is through quiet, focused prayer. In the busyness of life, it's easy to become distracted and forget to set aside time specifically for God. However, prophetic sensitivity thrives in environments of stillness and quiet. Psalm 46:10 reminds us,

> *"Be still and know that I am God."* NKJV

Stillness is not just the absence of noise; it's an intentional act of pausing and positioning your heart and mind to hear from God. In these quiet moments, God is able to speak to us through the gentle whispers of the Holy Spirit, and it is here that we can begin to recognize His subtle movements in our hearts and spirits.

This stillness allows us to tune into the small, often overlooked promptings of God, which are frequently drowned out by the noise and rush of daily life. When we create this space for God, we enable the Holy Spirit to move freely in our hearts and lives.

Alongside cultivating stillness, practicing responsiveness to the Holy Spirit's gentle nudges is key to developing greater sensitivity to God's voice. God speaks in many ways, and recognizing His voice requires us to be open and attentive to the variety of ways He communicates. These ways can include Scripture, impressions, inner thoughts, and even the quiet stirrings within our hearts.

The more we respond to these promptings—no matter how small—the more we attune ourselves to the Holy Spirit's direction. For example, you might feel prompted to pray for someone you've just met or offer an encouraging word to a friend. These small steps of obedience may seem insignificant at first, but over time they build trust in the process, and your ability to hear and respond to God's voice grows stronger.

Each time you act on these promptings, it reinforces your sensitivity to the Holy Spirit, and you begin to discern His voice with greater clarity. In addition to stillness and responsiveness, it's crucial to consistently test and weigh what you sense God is saying. The Holy Spirit will never lead you in a direction that contradicts His Word.

As you begin to sense God's promptings, it's important to test them against Scripture. This ensures that what you are hearing aligns with God's revealed truth and helps you avoid the risk of misinterpretation. For instance, if you sense a call to speak a prophetic word, ask yourself if it is consistent with the teachings of the Bible.

God's voice will always align with His Word, and when your promptings match Scripture, it confirms that you are on the right path. Testing what you hear against the Word also helps filter out distractions and ensures that your prophetic sensitivity is rooted in truth. Furthermore, God's voice is characterized by peace, clarity, and confirmation. Philippians 4:7 tells us,

> "And the peace of God, which transcends all understanding, will guard your hearts and minds in Christ Jesus." NIV

When God speaks, there is a sense of peace that accompanies His voice. It is not a voice of pressure, confusion, or condemnation, but one that brings reassurance and clarity. As you test the promptings you sense, take note of whether they bring peace to your heart. If a word or direction is filled with anxiety, fear, or confusion, it's a sign that it may not be from God.

God's voice always leads us to peace, and as you learn to recognize this peace, you will grow in confidence in discerning His voice. One practical way to develop this sensitivity is through journaling. As you spend time with God, take note of the promptings, impressions, and words you receive. Writing them down allows you to reflect on what God is saying and helps you track patterns in how He speaks to you.

Over time, this practice will strengthen your ability to discern His voice. Also, sharing these promptings with trusted mentors or fellow believers provides accountability and further confirmation. The more you test and weigh what you hear, the more you will be able to recognize God's voice with clarity and accuracy.

As you continue to practice responsiveness, stillness, and testing, you will find that your sensitivity to the Holy Spirit's promptings will increase. You will begin to recognize God's voice more clearly, not just in moments of prayer but in every aspect of your daily life. This growing sensitivity will allow you to speak more accurately on God's behalf, responding to His leadings with faith and confidence.

Just as a musician must practice regularly to refine their skills, so too must we practice attuning our hearts to God's voice. Over time, you will find that what once seemed like a challenge becomes second nature, and you will begin to walk in greater prophetic sensitivity, confidently responding to the Holy Spirit's promptings in every situation.

The Importance of Discernment

Discernment is a crucial gift for anyone who desires to walk in prophetic sensitivity, as it enables us to hear and recognize God's voice amidst the cacophony of competing messages that surround us daily. In a world filled with distractions, deceptions, and external pressures, the ability to distinguish between God's voice and other influences—whether our own thoughts, the enemy's lies, or the noise of culture—requires intentional development of our spiritual senses.

Prophetic discernment is not simply about knowing right from wrong; it's about being in tune with the Holy Spirit, who is the ultimate guide into all truth, and cultivating a heart that is aligned with God's will. The apostle John instructs us in 1 John 4:1 to:

"test the spirits to see whether they are from God," NIV

Emphasizing that not every thought or impression we experience is necessarily from God. This means that the prophetic voice requires careful testing, both against the truth of Scripture and the peace of the Holy Spirit, ensuring that what we hear is aligned with God's will. To develop discernment, one must first understand the nature of the Holy Spirit.

The Holy Spirit is our Helper, our Teacher, and our Guide. He is the one who leads us into all truth (John 16:13), and part of His role is to help us discern God's voice from the noise that competes for our attention. The more familiar we become with the Holy Spirit's presence, the clearer His voice becomes.

Just as we recognize the voice of a close friend or family member because of our relationship with them, we also become more adept at hearing God's voice as we spend more time with Him. Prayer, worship, and immersion in Scripture all play vital roles in this process.

When we invest in these practices, we train our hearts to recognize the subtleties of God's voice and the gentle nudges of the Holy Spirit. The more time we spend in God's presence, the more attuned we become to His voice, and the more we can discern His direction in our lives.

Another important avenue for developing discernment is through the community of believers. In the body of Christ, we are not meant to navigate the prophetic alone. The apostle Paul encourages us in 1 Corinthians 14:29 to,

"let two or three prophets speak, and let the others weigh what is said." ESV

This communal aspect of discernment ensures that prophetic words are tested, refined, and affirmed by the body of believers. Mature Christians, particularly those who are experienced in the prophetic, can offer valuable insights and guidance as you learn to discern God's voice. They can help you navigate the complexities of prophecy and offer correction when necessary, ensuring that you stay on track and avoid missteps.

There is great wisdom in seeking counsel from others who are further along in their journey, and this accountability strengthens the discernment process, protecting us from potential errors and guiding us toward greater clarity. As we continue to grow in discernment, we begin to recognize God's voice with greater accuracy and confidence. We become skilled at distinguishing between the voice of God and other competing voices —the voice of our own thoughts, the lies of the enemy, or the pressures of the world.

This increased clarity empowers us to speak with greater boldness, knowing that what we are hearing is truly from God. Additionally, as we develop the ability to discern God's voice more accurately, we also grow in understanding the deeper nuances of His heart. This allows us to speak not just general prophetic words, but words that are deeply aligned with God's specific purposes and plans for individuals, situations, or communities.

However, developing discernment is not a one-time process —it is an ongoing journey. It requires patience, humility, and a continual reliance on the Holy Spirit. Like any skill, it grows through practice and experience. The more we practice listening and responding to God's voice, the sharper our discernment becomes. Sometimes, this means stepping out in faith and learning through trial and error. But each step, whether a success or a lesson, contributes to our growth.

Over time, as we yield more fully to the Holy Spirit, our prophetic sensitivity sharpens, and we are better able to recognize and respond to God's voice with clarity and precision. One of the key aspects of discerning God's voice is recognizing the peace that accompanies it. In Philippians 4:7, we are promised that,

> "the peace of God, which transcends all understanding, will guard your hearts and minds in Christ Jesus." NIV

When we hear God's voice, it is often accompanied by a deep sense of peace and assurance. This peace is one of the most reliable indicators that what we are hearing is from God. The more we rely on the peace of the Holy Spirit as a guide, the more confident we become in discerning the truth.

Conversely, if there is confusion, anxiety, or a lack of peace, it may be a signal that the message is not from God, or that further discernment is needed. Ultimately, discernment is about more than just recognizing God's voice—it's about aligning our hearts with His will and learning to respond to His guidance with obedience and trust.

It requires an ongoing relationship with the Holy Spirit, who helps us navigate the complexities of hearing from God. As we grow in discernment, we begin to speak and act with greater boldness, knowing that we are hearing God's heart and delivering His message to those around us.

Prophetic sensitivity, then, is a lifelong journey of deepening intimacy with God, continual reliance on the Holy Spirit, and growing confidence in discerning His voice. The more we yield to His voice, the sharper our discernment becomes, and the more effectively we can walk in prophetic sensitivity, speaking God's truth and love to the world around us.

Developing prophetic sensitivity is a journey of growth and learning, and it requires intentional practices, consistent prayer, and a willingness to step out in faith. The Holy Spirit plays a central role in this process, guiding, empowering, and sharpening our ability to hear God's voice clearly.

Through time spent in stillness, responsive obedience, and tested discernment, we can cultivate a life of prophetic sensitivity that allows us to speak the words of God with confidence and love. As we continue to grow in sensitivity to God's voice, we will be better equipped to minister prophetically, hearing and responding to His heart for those around us.

Reflection Questions

1. What steps can you take to create more opportunities for stillness and quietness in your daily life to better hear God's voice?
2. How can you distinguish between the voice of the Holy Spirit and other influences, such as your own thoughts or external distractions?

Activations

1. **Quiet Listening Exercise:** Spend 10 minutes in complete silence, focusing on tuning your heart to God. Ask the Holy Spirit to speak to you during this time. Write down any impressions, words, or scriptures that come to mind, even if they seem small or insignificant. Reflect on how you feel and what you sense during this quiet time.
2. **Responding to a Prompting:** During your day, ask the Holy Spirit to give you a specific prompting, such as encouraging someone, praying for a need, or sharing a scripture. Act immediately when you sense a nudge, no matter how small it seems, and note the outcome. Journal how you felt before and after responding to His prompting.
3. **Testing and Discerning an Impression:** Reflect on a recent thought, dream, or word you felt was from God. Take time to pray and compare it to Scripture. Share it with a trusted spiritual mentor for confirmation and feedback. Observe how peace or clarity accompanies this process, and document your insights.

CHAPTER 4
PROPHECY AND THE WORD OF GOD

In the prophetic ministry, the Word of God is the unshakable foundation upon which all prophetic words should be built. Prophecy is never meant to stand alone; it is always an extension of God's eternal truth, designed to reveal His heart, encourage His people, and guide them toward His will. The key to understanding how prophecy aligns with Scripture is recognizing that prophetic revelation never contradicts God's revealed Word.

Prophecy exists to point us back to God's truth, bringing further understanding and clarity, never to alter or override the timeless principles He has already established in the Bible. This chapter will explore how prophecy should always be rooted in Scripture, how it must align with the heart of God's Word, and how we can use the Bible to confirm and test prophetic words.

The Importance of Being Rooted in Scripture

When we begin to understand prophecy's role in the life of the believer, we first need to grasp the importance of being deeply rooted in Scripture. The Bible is God's final and unchanging Word to us. Every prophetic word must align with it, as it holds the complete counsel of God for all matters of life.

Prophecy is not meant to be a replacement for Scripture, but rather a living expression of God's Word that brings specific application to our current lives, bringing clarity to what has already been revealed. Just as Jesus responded to the enemy's temptations in the wilderness by quoting Scripture (Matthew 4:1-11), so should we always measure prophetic words against the standard of God's written Word.

This practice ensures that any word spoken is aligned with God's unchanging truth. As believers, we must saturate our hearts and minds with the Word of God so that we can discern any word spoken in the prophetic realm that may be contrary to it. A word from God will never contradict what He has already said in Scripture.

The more intimately we know God's Word, the sharper our ability to recognize what is from Him and what is not. Prophetic words should feel familiar to us, like a deeper revelation of the very same Word we read in Scripture.

The apostle Paul's reminder to Timothy that "all Scripture is inspired by God" (2 Timothy 3:16) serves as a reminder that the prophetic word will always work hand in hand with God's written Word to correct, teach, and build us up. If a prophecy feels off or contradictory to Scripture, *it should be questioned and tested with great care.*

How Prophecy Should Always Align with God's Revealed Word

The Bible is the foundation of all spiritual truth, and prophecy cannot stand outside of its bounds. If we receive a prophetic word, it should never contradict or add anything to the doctrines that are clearly laid out in Scripture. A prophetic word may bring new insights or personal revelation, but it should always align with the character and nature of God as revealed through His Word.

Prophetic words that lead us away from the principles laid out in Scripture—such as calls to disobedience, self-centeredness, or immorality—are not from God. The prophetic is meant to uplift the believer into deeper alignment with God's purposes, not to contradict the moral and ethical teachings found in the Bible.

For example, a word calling someone to act in sin or compromise would never be from the Holy Spirit, as God's Word is clear about His will for holiness. Moreover, prophecy is not meant to redefine the message of the Gospel. It doesn't alter the life, death, and resurrection of Jesus Christ or the salvation available through Him.

If a prophetic word seems to shift focus from the core of the Gospel or present another gospel, it must be rejected. Prophecy always confirms and supports the message of Jesus Christ, aligning with God's will to glorify Him through salvation, sanctification, and the work of the Holy Spirit.

Using Scripture to Confirm Prophetic Words

One of the greatest ways to test whether a prophetic word is from God is to use Scripture as a measure. Prophecy should resonate with the heart of the Scriptures and never depart from the revelation that has been given through God's Word. In practical terms, this means that when you receive a prophetic word, you should ask: "Does this align with the character of God as seen in the Bible? Does it line up with the principles that Jesus laid out for us?"

Scripture serves as a confirmation in the process of discernment. It does not necessarily have to be a direct verse-for-verse confirmation, but the essence of the prophetic word will always line up with the spirit of God's Word. When God speaks through prophecy, He is not bringing something new that contradicts His previous revelation; He is simply shining new light on it, helping us apply His Word to our specific situation.

For instance, if you receive a word of encouragement, it may be confirmed by passages such as Isaiah 40:31, where God promises strength to those who wait on Him. If you receive a word of correction, it should align with Scriptures like Hebrews 12, which speaks of God's discipline and correction as an expression of His love. These confirmations within Scripture give confidence that the word we have received is not only prophetic but also rooted in God's eternal truth.

The Holy Spirit plays a significant role in this process, offering an inner witness of peace when the prophetic word is truly from God. This inner witness, alongside the confirmation found in Scripture, provides a strong foundation for trusting that what has been spoken aligns with God's will.

The Role of Scripture in Prophetic Training

For those seeking to grow in the prophetic ministry, Scripture is essential to our training and maturity. The more we immerse ourselves in the Word of God, the more equipped we are to hear His voice clearly and accurately. Prophetic training isn't just about developing a sensitivity to the Holy Spirit's promptings; it's also about knowing God's Word deeply so we can confidently test and confirm what we hear.

Understanding Scripture helps us recognize the kinds of words God speaks and how He uses prophecy in the lives of His people. It teaches us what to expect from prophetic ministry and helps us to discern when something doesn't align with the character of God. Prophetic words should never be isolated from the body of biblical truth but should always reflect God's heart as revealed through His Word.

As we grow in our prophetic gift, we must continually refine our ability to align what we hear with the written Word of God. This practice ensures that we are not led astray by our own desires, misinterpretations, or external influences but remain firmly anchored in the truth of God's revealed Word.

The relationship between prophecy and the Word of God is one of deep unity and mutual confirmation. Prophecy is a powerful tool for building up the church and guiding believers into deeper intimacy with God, but it must always align with the truth revealed in Scripture. As we continue to grow in our prophetic gift, it is crucial that we remain deeply rooted in God's Word, constantly testing and confirming what we hear against the standard of Scripture.

By doing so, we ensure that our prophetic words not only bring life and encouragement but also stand as faithful reflections of God's eternal truth, pointing His people back to His heart and His will.

Reflection Questions

1. How does your current understanding of Scripture influence your ability to discern prophetic words? Reflect on how deeply you are rooted in God's Word and identify areas where you can grow in biblical knowledge to better test and confirm prophecy.
2. Have you ever received a prophetic word that didn't fully align with Scripture? How did you handle it, and what steps did you take to ensure your response was rooted in God's truth?

Activations

1. **Scripture-Prophecy Alignment Exercise:** Spend time meditating on a passage of Scripture (e.g., 2 Timothy 3:16-17 or Matthew 4:4). Then, ask the Holy Spirit to speak to you prophetically through that passage. Write down what you hear and compare it with the Scripture to ensure alignment. Share your reflections with a trusted spiritual mentor for feedback.
2. **Prophetic Word Testing Activation:** Think of a prophetic word you have received or given in the past. Use the following steps to test it:
   - Find at least two Scriptures that confirm or align with the word.
   - Pray and ask the Holy Spirit for further clarity or peace about the word.
   - Evaluate how the word reflects the character and principles of God as revealed in the Bible.

Journal your findings and consider how this process strengthens your discernment in the prophetic ministry.

CHAPTER 5
THE HEART OF PROPHECY

In the prophetic journey, it's crucial to recognize that prophecy is not merely a spiritual gift—it's a powerful conduit of God's heart, meant to release His love and honor into the lives of His people. As we step into the flow of prophecy, we must remember that the very essence of prophetic ministry is to align our hearts with the heartbeat of God, and it is always motivated by love.

The delivery of prophetic words should come from a place of deep respect for God's people and be a reflection of His character. This chapter emphasizes the importance of love and honor in prophetic ministry, offering insights into how we can grow in these areas, ensuring that our prophetic voices speak life and hope.

Prophecy Must Flow from a Place of Love

The apostle Paul challenges us with a powerful truth in 1 Corinthians 13:2, saying,

> "If I have the gift of prophecy and can fathom all mysteries and all

knowledge, and if I have a faith that can move mountains, but do not have love, I am nothing." NIV

This scripture calls us back to the fundamental purpose of prophecy: to serve as a reflection of God's love. Without love, even the most accurate, powerful prophetic words can miss the mark, as they lack the divine heartbeat behind them. Prophecy is never about impressing others or showcasing our spiritual insights.

At its core, prophecy is meant to build up, edify, and comfort those who hear it. It's about releasing God's love into someone's life, bringing healing, hope, and a deeper understanding of His heart. When prophecy is rooted in love, it becomes a channel of transformation, shifting the atmosphere and bringing life where there was once discouragement.

True prophecy carries the fragrance of God's love, softening hearts and drawing them closer to Him. A prophetic word devoid of love can easily become harsh, critical, or even manipulative. It can wound instead of heal, and in some cases, it may push people away from the very God it was meant to reveal.

Prophetic ministry must therefore be constantly examined in light of God's love—this ensures that our words are tools of life, not instruments of destruction.

Honoring God and Others When Delivering Prophetic Words

When we step into prophetic ministry, we must remember that we are representing God. The prophetic word we deliver is not just for the individual but is a message from the Creator Himself. Therefore, our words must honor God's character—

reflecting His goodness, kindness, and gentleness. Honoring God means delivering words with a sense of awe, reverence, and responsibility, knowing that we are His vessels in the earth.

Moreover, prophecy is not just a message to be delivered—it's a message meant to bless others. When we deliver prophetic words, we are called to honor those to whom the word is given. Honoring others means considering their dignity and emotional state before we speak. It means recognizing the timing and the method—whether the word should be spoken publicly or privately.

Prophecy is not a weapon to wield for our own agendas but a divine tool meant to serve the people of God, pointing them toward His love and purpose. Honor in prophetic ministry also includes a deep respect for the sovereignty of the individual's will. We never use prophecy to control or manipulate others into making decisions.

Instead, we speak words that align with God's will, empowering the person to act in faith and alignment with God's purposes. The prophetic word should always leave room for the individual to respond in obedience, not out of pressure or fear.

Avoiding Manipulation or Control in Prophetic Ministry

One of the greatest dangers in prophetic ministry is the temptation to use the gift for control, manipulation, or personal gain. Some may be tempted to deliver prophetic words that pressurize individuals into making decisions that align with the prophet's own agenda. However, prophetic ministry should always be a servant-hearted expression, aimed at lifting others up, never at creating dependence or forcing action.

True prophecy is always given with an open hand, not an iron grip. It never comes with the weight of expectation or demand. Instead, it leaves space for people to choose how they will respond. Prophetic ministry is about speaking what God has revealed, not manipulating others into a particular outcome. It is not about controlling the actions of others but about giving them the clarity and insight they need to hear from God for themselves.

It is crucial to remember that God's voice is a voice of peace. It's one that brings clarity, not confusion. If a prophetic word brings pressure, fear, or confusion, it may not be from God. God's voice always encourages freedom of choice and provides the peace necessary to respond in faith. As prophetic vessels, our role is to partner with the Holy Spirit in releasing God's heart with wisdom and discernment.

Humility in Prophetic Ministry

Humility is the cornerstone of prophetic ministry. When we are humble in the prophetic, we recognize that we are simply messengers, not the source of the message. It is a grace-filled ministry, not one based on our own efforts or abilities. The prophet's role is to speak what God is saying, with no agenda other than to see His will come to pass.

Humility also means that we must be willing to submit our words to the leadership of the local church. Prophetic ministry should always be practiced in the context of the body of Christ, under the covering and guidance of spiritual leaders. This submission ensures that the prophetic ministry is kept healthy and aligned with the overall vision and purpose of the church. The humble prophet does not seek their own platform, but desires to serve the greater good of God's Kingdom.

In addition, humility in prophetic ministry means being open to correction and growth. Prophetic ministry is not about perfection but about growing in intimacy with God and in understanding His ways. A humble prophet is teachable, ready to learn, and willing to adjust their understanding as they grow in the gift.

The Role of Love and Honor in Corporate Prophetic Ministry

In corporate settings, prophecy should be delivered with a strong sense of love and honor. The role of the prophet in a gathered assembly is not to dominate or control, but to serve the body of Christ. Prophetic words should bring unity, not division. They should encourage, not discourage.

As we deliver words in a group setting, it's vital that we ensure our delivery is respectful, considerate, and aligned with God's purposes for the group. When prophecy is delivered in love and honor, it creates a culture of expectation and faith. People are encouraged to step into the prophetic flow themselves, and the entire church body becomes edified. A prophetic culture based on love and honor cultivates an environment where God's presence is welcomed, and His voice is heard clearly.

Prophecy as a Reflection of God's Heart

At its deepest level, prophecy is not simply a gift or a tool for revealing the future—it is a powerful reflection of God's heart. It's an expression of His love for His people and His desire to see them flourish. As we grow in prophetic ministry, we must remain rooted in love and honor, allowing these qualities to shape the words we speak and the way we deliver them.

True prophetic ministry is marked by humility, respect, and a deep desire to see God's will accomplished. When prophecy flows from love and honor, it becomes a transformative force, bringing healing, restoration, and clarity to the body of Christ. It is not about the prophet or the prophecy—it is about releasing God's heart into the world, and seeing His Kingdom come.

Reflection Questions

1. How does prioritizing love and honor in prophetic ministry influence the way we deliver and receive prophetic words?
2. In what ways can humility safeguard prophetic ministry from becoming manipulative or self-serving?

Activations

1. **Love-Centered Prophetic Practice:** Spend time in prayer asking God to reveal His heart of love for a specific person. Write down what you sense Him saying and intentionally focus on speaking words that build, edify, and encourage them. Then, deliver the word with gentleness and respect.
2. **Honor in Action:** Choose someone you've felt prompted to encourage prophetically. Before speaking, ask God for insight into how to deliver the message in a way that honors their current emotional state and spiritual journey. Share the word with a focus on timing, tone, and God's kindness.

CHAPTER 6
HOW TO DELIVER A PROPHETIC WORD

Delivering a prophetic word is not just a matter of communicating information—it's a sacred act of obedience to God and a responsibility that requires wisdom, humility, and discernment. Prophecy is a powerful tool through which God reveals His heart to His people. However, the way we deliver a prophetic word is just as important as the word itself.

It is essential to ensure that the message is conveyed with clarity, sensitivity, and in alignment with the heart of God. In this chapter, we will dive deep into the practical steps for delivering prophetic words, the nuances of timing, tone, and approach, and how to handle both public and private settings.

Practical Steps for Delivering a Prophetic Word with Wisdom and Clarity

1. **Pray and Seek Clarity:** Before delivering any prophetic word, take time to pray and ensure that you're hearing from God. It's easy to confuse our own thoughts with God's voice, so it's important to seek confirmation through prayer and journal-

ing. If the word is unclear, ask God for further revelation. This is not just about accuracy—it's about speaking from His heart. Prophetic words should always be birthed from a place of prayer and intimacy with God. The clearer the word, the greater the impact it will have.

> • **A Prophetic Word is First Received in Prayer:** Spending time in prayer prepares the heart to hear and discern clearly. James 1:5 tells us that if we lack wisdom, we should ask of God. So, when stepping out to deliver a prophetic word, ask God to give you wisdom, clarity, and understanding. Pray that He will bring understanding to both the hearer and the speaker.

2. Test the Word Before You Speak: Always test the word before you deliver it, particularly if it's significant or has the potential to bring correction. The word must align with Scripture and the character of God. Prophecy should never contradict the Bible, but should always be in line with the principles and truths of God's Word. If you feel hesitant or unsure, seek confirmation through a mentor or trusted spiritual leader. It's important to develop an understanding of God's nature so that you can test the word accurately and in the right spirit.

> • **Test the Fruit:** Every prophetic word should bear fruit consistent with the character of God—peace, love, encouragement, and correction that leads to restoration. A good test is to ask: "What is the fruit of this word? Is it bringing edification or confusion?"

3. Be Specific and Clear: When delivering a prophetic word, specificity is key. Vague or generalized words can often cause confusion or lead to misinterpretation. God speaks with precision, and the prophetic word should reflect that. Speak in a way that clearly communicates God's heart for the individual, the church, or the situation. A word that is direct and clear carries authority because it's coming from a place of confidence in what God is saying. Avoid using obscure language that could dilute the message.

4. Speak from a Place of Love: Prophetic words are not just messages to be conveyed—they are expressions of God's love and care. When you deliver a prophetic word, it should be drenched in love. Even if the word involves correction or rebuke, it must be done in love. When prophecy is rooted in love, it builds up, encourages, and strengthens. God's heart in prophecy is always to restore, never to destroy.

- **Prophecy as an Invitation, Not a Judgment:** Prophecy is an invitation to align with God's will, not a tool to shame or control. Prophetic words should always be delivered in the spirit of invitation, drawing people closer to God and to His purposes for their lives.

5. Check Your Motive: Before delivering a prophetic word, ensure that your motive is pure. Prophecy should never be used for personal gain, control, or manipulation. It's not about impressing others or elevating your own spiritual status. Prophecy is an act of service to the body of Christ. Check your heart and make sure that your motive is to see God's will accomplished in the lives of those you are speaking to.

- **Guard Your Heart:** The Bible tells us that out of the heart, the mouth speaks (Matthew 12:34). Make sure your heart is aligned with God's love, and that your words are intended to edify and encourage, not to elevate yourself or manipulate others.

Timing, Tone, and Approach in Prophecy

1. **Recognize the Right Timing:** Timing is critical when delivering a prophetic word. A word spoken at the wrong time can cause confusion or even harm. Often, the right word at the wrong time is ineffective. It's essential to be in tune with the Holy Spirit to know when to speak and when to remain silent. God's timing is always perfect, and delivering a word at the appropriate moment can make all the difference.

- **Wait for the Holy Spirit's Release:** Sometimes, God gives us a word, but we must wait for the right moment to deliver it. The Holy Spirit will prompt us when the time is right. He will also give us the grace to wait until the person is ready to hear the word. If you're unsure, ask the Holy Spirit to lead you in His timing.

2. **Tone of Voice:** The tone in which you deliver a prophetic word is just as important as the content. A harsh tone can hinder the message, while a gentle tone can draw the person's heart closer to the message. Tone should reflect the nature of the word. If it's a word of comfort, your tone should be soothing and gentle. If it's a word of correction, your tone should still be full of grace and humility.

- **Speak with Compassion and Tenderness:** Even when delivering words of challenge or rebuke, make sure your tone reflects the compassion and tenderness of God. A word given in the wrong tone can create fear, defensiveness, or resistance. God's voice is loving and kind, and our tone should reflect that.

3. **Private vs. Public Delivery:** There's a difference between delivering a prophetic word publicly and privately. Public

words are usually more general and are intended for the congregation or the larger body of believers. These words should encourage and build up the church, often focusing on corporate vision, direction, or encouragement.

- **Public Prophecy**: When delivering a word in a public setting, such as a church service, make sure the word is edifying to the entire body. Avoid personal or overly specific words that might disrupt the flow of worship or cause confusion. Public words should carry an anointing that resonates with the whole group, offering encouragement or conviction where needed.

- **Private Prophecy**: Personal words often have a more intimate and specific tone. In private settings, you may speak directly to an individual, sharing insight into their personal circumstances, direction, or struggles. These words require sensitivity and confidentiality, and they should be delivered with care, ensuring the person feels loved and encouraged.

4. **Delivering Words in Love and Humility**: Prophetic words are not about showing off our spiritual gift, but about revealing God's heart for His people. Always deliver words with humility, recognizing that you are simply a vessel for God's message. When you speak from a place of humility, it reflects the true nature of God's voice—He is kind, loving, and merciful.

- **A Humble Heart**: Remember that you are a steward of the prophetic gift, not its owner. Prophecy is not a platform for self-promotion, but a tool for God's glory. Approach every word you deliver with a humble heart and a desire to see God's will accomplished.

Key Guidelines for Delivering Prophecy

1. Be Encouraging and Edifying: 1 Corinthians 14:3 says that prophecy is meant to edify, encourage, and comfort. Even if the word contains correction or challenge, it should ultimately point to God's purpose for the individual or group. Prophetic words should never bring shame, guilt, or condemnation. They should always be an invitation to step into God's purposes for their life.

- **Speak Life:** God's prophetic voice brings life. When you deliver a prophetic word, aim to speak life over individuals, even in challenging circumstances. Your words should stir faith, encourage hope, and empower people to walk into their destiny.

2. Practice Accountability: While prophecy is personal, it should always be delivered in a way that invites accountability. Every prophetic word, whether public or private, should be tested, especially when it carries significant weight. In the church setting, prophetic words should be submitted to the leadership for discernment and accountability.

- **Submit to Leadership:** When giving prophetic words in a corporate setting, it's important to submit those words to leadership for confirmation and prayer. This creates a safe and healthy environment for prophecy to function properly and protects the integrity of the prophetic ministry.

3. Respond to Resistance with Grace: Not every prophetic word will be readily accepted. Some may meet with resistance or doubt. If this happens, don't be discouraged. Respond with grace and allow God to work in His timing. Sometimes, prophetic words need time to be understood or received, especially when they challenge people's comfort zones or perceptions.

4. Invite the Holy Spirit's Presence: Above all, prophecy should invite the Holy Spirit's presence and power into the situation. We are not just delivering words; we are creating an environment where God's spirit can move and transform. Ask the Holy Spirit to confirm, convict, and empower those who hear the prophetic word to respond in faith and obedience.

The Power of Prophecy Delivered with Wisdom and Love

The delivery of a prophetic word is a moment of divine partnership with God, where His voice is expressed through you to build, encourage, and equip His people. When we deliver a word with wisdom, love, and humility, it not only brings clarity but also draws people closer to God's heart.

Prophecy is an incredible privilege and responsibility. When done correctly, it strengthens the body of Christ, provides direction, and fosters intimacy with the Holy Spirit. As you grow in your understanding and delivery of prophetic words, remember that you are a vessel of God's voice, called to edify, encourage, and equip the body of Christ for His purposes.

Reflection Questions

1. How do you ensure that your prophetic words are aligned with God's character and Scripture before delivering them?
2. In what ways can your tone, timing, or motive enhance or hinder the impact of a prophetic word?

Activation Steps

1. Spend intentional time in prayer this week, asking God to give you clarity and wisdom for any prophetic words He may want you to deliver. Journal any impressions or words you receive and test them against Scripture before sharing.
2. Practice delivering a prophetic word to a trusted mentor or spiritual leader for feedback. Focus on clarity, love, and humility, and ask for guidance on how you can grow in this area.

CHAPTER 7
TESTING AND JUDGING PROPHETIC WORDS

In the journey of prophecy, one of the most important principles to grasp is the biblical mandate to test and judge prophetic words. Not every word that is spoken or received is from God. The Scriptures are clear:

> *"Do not despise prophecies, but test everything; hold fast what is good"* (1 Thessalonians 5:20-21) ESV

This call to discernment and responsibility in handling prophetic words is vital for every believer who desires to walk in the fullness of God's prophetic calling.

The Biblical Mandate for Testing Prophecy

Testing prophetic words is not just a suggestion; it is an essential part of walking in spiritual maturity and protecting the integrity of the prophetic ministry. Prophecy is not infallible; it is a gift given to imperfect vessels, and thus, it must be examined in light of Scripture, personal discernment, and the community of believers. Just as the Berean's,

> *"received the word with all eagerness, examining the Scriptures daily to see if these things were so"* (Acts 17:11) ESV

We must approach prophecy with a heart of humility and a desire for truth. Testing prophecy ensures that we are stewarding God's voice responsibly. In a world filled with competing voices, the ability to discern truth from error is more critical than ever.

As a believer, you must be equipped to recognize if a word aligns with the heart and character of God. The Word of God, the Spirit of God, and the community of believers all serve as the lenses through which prophecy is to be tested and evaluated.

How to Discern If a Word is From God

Discernment is at the core of testing prophetic words. It's essential to develop an intimate relationship with the Holy Spirit, for it is the Spirit who helps us test and judge the authenticity of a prophetic word. Prophetic words must be tested against Scripture. This is non-negotiable. If the word contradicts the written Word of God, it cannot be from God.

The consistency of God's voice throughout Scripture is unchanging, and prophecy will never contradict the foundations of the Bible. One of the most common ways the Holy Spirit speaks is through the peace of God. When a prophetic word is spoken, one of the first things to check is the inner witness of peace.

Does the word bring a sense of peace, or does it stir anxiety and confusion? If peace is absent, it may be an indication that the word needs to be reevaluated. The word must also align with the nature and character of God. The prophetic gift is designed to edify, exhort, and comfort (1 Corinthians 14:3). If a word brings condemnation, shame, or confusion, it likely does not originate from the Lord. His voice always leads us to greater hope, transformation, and encouragement.

Prophecy Is Often Conditional

One critical aspect of prophecy that is often misunderstood is that prophetic words can be conditional. Just because a word is received from God does not mean it is an absolute, unchangeable declaration. Many times, prophecy serves as an invitation to partner with God in bringing about His will on the earth.

Prophetic words can reveal God's heart and His intentions, but they often require faith and obedience to see them come to pass. In 1 Timothy 1:18-19*, Paul encouraged Timothy to, *"wage the good warfare"* with the prophecies spoken over him. This reveals the dynamic nature of prophecy—it is a spiritual weapon that requires action.

The prophetic word can be like a seed that needs watering, faith to be stirred, and obedience to be activated. If you receive a prophetic word, it's important to understand that it may involve a process, sometimes requiring us to step into it with boldness and faith.

Additionally, some prophetic words come with conditions. For example, God may promise something over your life but add that it will happen if you remain faithful, if you repent, or if you align with His will. This is not a contradiction but rather an

---

* NKJV

invitation to cooperate with God's purpose in your life. God's promises are sure, but they often require our active participation.

The Role of Prophetic Accountability

Accountability in the prophetic is an often-neglected but essential part of the prophetic process. Testing and judging prophecy should never be a solo endeavor. Prophetic words are meant to be submitted to the community for confirmation and accountability.

There is wisdom in a multitude of counselors (Proverbs 15:22), and prophetic words should be weighed carefully in the company of mature believers. When testing a prophetic word, seek the counsel of others who are spiritually mature. Share the word with leaders you trust and who have a proven track record of spiritual discernment.

Prophecy should always be submitted to the authority of the local church, as they are the ones entrusted with the oversight of the body of Christ. When prophetic words are shared in community, the body can collectively discern the validity and application of the word.

This accountability ensures that we do not walk in isolation or pride but remain grounded in humility and in the wisdom of those who have walked the prophetic journey before us. As Proverbs 27:17 says, "Iron sharpens iron," and so does the healthy exchange of prophetic words within the community of believers.

Moving Forward with Wisdom

When a prophetic word has been tested and found to be from God, there is a responsibility to steward that word wisely. There may be a season of waiting, preparing, or positioning yourself to see the fulfillment of the word. While prophecy can give us a glimpse into God's heart, it is often up to us to take steps of faith and obedience to see it fulfilled.

The process of testing and judging prophetic words may not always be immediate or easy, but it is a necessary part of growing in prophetic maturity. The more we practice discernment, the more we grow in our ability to recognize God's voice and understand His timing. We must remember that prophecy is a gift, but it is a gift that must be stewarded with care, humility, and reverence.

Testing and judging prophetic words are vital to maintaining the integrity of the prophetic ministry and to ensuring that we walk in the fullness of what God desires to speak through us. As believers, we are called to test, discern, and align ourselves with God's voice, so that His will is accomplished in and through our lives. By remaining faithful, humble, and discerning, we can become more accurate vessels of God's prophetic heart in the world today.

Reflection Questions

1. How can you actively cultivate a deeper sensitivity to the Holy Spirit to discern whether a prophetic word is from God?
2. In what ways can you invite accountability from spiritual leaders and your community when testing prophetic words in your life?

Activations

1. **Testing a Word:** Reflect on a prophetic word you have received in the past. Take time to examine it against Scripture, seek the inner witness of peace, and ask trusted spiritual leaders for their counsel. Write down what you sense God is affirming and any steps He may be calling you to take.
2. **Scripture Alignment Practice:** Choose a recent or hypothetical prophetic word and compare it to at least three specific Scriptures to discern its alignment with God's character and promises. Pray for wisdom and journal your findings, noting how this exercise strengthens your discernment.

CHAPTER 8
COMMON PITFALLS IN THE PROPHETIC

Prophecy is one of the most powerful and transformative gifts in the body of Christ, yet it comes with its own set of challenges. As believers who operate in the prophetic, we must be aware of common pitfalls that can hinder our effectiveness, authenticity, and integrity in delivering God's messages.

In this chapter, we will explore several pitfalls that prophets must be cautious of, and we will learn how to overcome them through humility, wisdom, and grace.

Avoiding Pride, Presumption, and Striving

One of the most dangerous traps a prophetic person can fall into is the temptation of pride. Pride often manifests when we begin to believe that our prophetic gift is about us rather than about God and His people. We may start to take ownership of the words God gives us, seeking recognition or validation for our abilities.

Prophets must guard their hearts against the spirit of self-glorification. The prophetic gift is not meant to elevate us, but to elevate God and bring His kingdom into greater alignment on earth. It's also important to avoid presumption, where we step out in the prophetic without a clear word from God.

Presumption arises when we begin to operate in the prophetic out of our own desires or assumptions, rather than waiting on God's timing and guidance. Prophets who presume too much may begin to speak from their own thoughts or imagination rather than from God's heart.

This can lead to confusion, error, and even damage to those we seek to serve. Striving is another pitfall that often accompanies prophetic ministry. The prophetic gift is not something we need to force or make happen—it is an overflow of our relationship with God.

When we strive to prove ourselves or to fulfill an expectation, we can easily move out of the grace of God and fall into works of the flesh. Prophecy should come from a place of rest and intimacy with God, not from a place of striving to perform or impress others.

Dealing with Fear of Man and Fear of Getting It Wrong

Fear of man is a common struggle for many who are called to the prophetic. As we are called to deliver words that may challenge, encourage, or even correct others, the fear of rejection or ridicule can creep in. This fear causes us to hesitate or second-guess the words we feel God is giving us, and it can lead us to withhold the very message that God wants to release through us.

It's important to remember that the prophetic is about

obedience to God, not the approval of men. We must learn to prioritize God's opinion over people's opinions, knowing that we are accountable to Him alone. When we focus on pleasing God, we can step out in faith with boldness and clarity, regardless of how our words might be received.

The fear of getting it wrong can also paralyze prophetic voices. We may fear that if we miss it or misunderstand God's voice, we will be discredited or seen as unreliable. However, we must recognize that no prophetic voice is infallible. Prophecy is not about perfection but about partnership with the Holy Spirit.

While we should strive for accuracy, we must also cultivate an atmosphere of grace where mistakes are opportunities for growth, not for condemnation. The more we step out in faith, the more we will fine-tune our ability to hear and deliver God's voice.

Learning from Mistakes Without Quitting

One of the greatest hindrances to growth in the prophetic is the fear of failure. Prophetic people who make mistakes—whether it be misinterpreting a word or delivering it poorly—can be discouraged and tempted to quit altogether. However, prophetic ministry is a journey of learning and growing.

Each mistake is an opportunity to refine our ability to hear from God and communicate His heart more clearly. When we make a mistake, we must not allow shame or condemnation to rule over us. Instead, we must approach our mistakes with humility, recognizing that we are all on a learning curve.

God is not surprised by our failures, and He is always ready to teach us through them. The key is to stay teachable, to seek guidance from mature mentors, and to use each experience as a stepping stone toward greater clarity and effectiveness in our prophetic calling.

Prophets should also learn to apologize and correct any damage caused by incorrect words. When our prophetic words miss the mark or cause confusion, it's important to acknowledge the mistake, ask for forgiveness if necessary, and take responsibility. This humility will build trust and integrity in our prophetic ministry and will honor the people we are called to serve.

Avoiding the pitfalls in the prophetic is not about perfection, but about cultivating a heart of humility, sensitivity, and obedience to the Holy Spirit. By guarding against pride, presumption, striving, fear of man, and the fear of making mistakes, we create space for God to speak through us with greater clarity and authority.

As we learn from our missteps and continue to grow in our prophetic journey, we become more effective vessels for releasing God's heart into the world—edifying, exhorting, and comforting those who are hungry for His voice.

Reflection Questions

1. How have pride, fear of man, or the fear of making mistakes impacted your ability to walk confidently in your prophetic calling?
2. When you make a mistake in prophetic ministry, how can you respond in a way that reflects humility and a willingness to grow?

Activations

1. **Heart Check:** Spend time in prayer asking the Holy Spirit to reveal any areas where pride, striving, or fear may have influenced your prophetic ministry. Journal what He shows you, and ask Him for grace to move forward with humility and boldness.
2. **Bold Obedience:** Identify one prophetic word or impression you've recently received but hesitated to share out of fear. Submit it to trusted spiritual mentors for discernment and, if affirmed, deliver it in obedience to God, focusing on faith rather than fear of man.

CHAPTER 9
PROPHETIC PROTOCOL IN THE LOCAL CHURCH

Prophecy is a powerful tool given by God to His Church to edify, encourage, and bring comfort. As believers, we are all called to participate in this ministry, but when prophecy is practiced within a corporate setting, it must be done with order and respect for both God's guidance and the spiritual health of the congregation. The importance of prophetic protocol cannot be overstated.

In this chapter, we will explore how prophecy should function within the local church, with an emphasis on submission to leadership, maintaining the health of the body, and creating a culture that embraces the prophetic gift.

The Role of Prophecy in Corporate Worship

Prophecy within the context of corporate worship serves a unique and vital purpose. It is not simply about declaring future events but about creating an atmosphere where God's presence is invited, His heart is revealed, and His people are drawn closer to Him.

Prophetic words in worship can encourage those who are weary, convict those who are living in sin, and bring direction to a congregation that is seeking God's will. As the prophetic is released during worship, the focus must remain on glorifying God and uplifting His people.

Prophecy should not disrupt the flow of the service but rather complement the spirit of worship that is already present. Prophetic words that align with the atmosphere of the service will help steer hearts and minds toward God's intended purpose, whether it be a call to repentance, a declaration of victory, or an invitation into deeper intimacy with Him.

A key element of the prophetic in corporate worship is the understanding that it's not about one person standing out or drawing attention to themselves. It's about creating a space where God speaks to His people. Prophets must remember that their role is to serve, not to perform. The prophetic word must always be presented in humility and with a heart that desires to glorify God, not the messenger.

While prophecy can be spontaneous in worship, it must be stewarded with wisdom. Prophetic words should always reflect God's nature—His character of love, mercy, and truth. Just as a song of worship flows smoothly from one melody to the next, so should the prophetic move through a service in a seamless, spirit-led way.

Worship leaders and prophetic voices must work together to create an atmosphere conducive to receiving God's revelation, where the hearts of the congregation are open to hearing from Him. The prophetic is not a stand-alone ministry but is integral to the flow of corporate worship, where each element enhances the other.

Submitting Prophetic Words to Church Leadership

Submission to leadership is a foundational principle in all aspects of the Christian life, and this includes the prophetic ministry. In the local church, prophetic words should be submitted to the church leadership for discernment, testing, and confirmation.

This submission ensures that prophetic words align with the overall vision and direction of the church and are in harmony with biblical truth. Submission does not diminish the authority of the prophetic voice; rather, it provides accountability, protection, and wisdom.

Leaders are called to shepherd the flock, and part of their responsibility is to oversee and steward the prophetic words that are released within the church. They are tasked with discerning whether the word aligns with scripture, whether it brings edification, exhortation, and comfort, and whether it is in line with the needs of the body.

Prophetic individuals should never be discouraged by this process of submission. In fact, it is an opportunity for growth and maturity in their calling. Prophets must embrace accountability with grace, knowing that this is a safeguard for both their personal ministry and the health of the church as a whole.

The church leadership, on the other hand, must approach prophetic words with discernment, humility, and prayer, recognizing that the Holy Spirit speaks through many vessels, each with their own unique perspective. This relationship between the prophetic and church leadership ensures that the local body of believers is protected from any false or inaccurate words.

Leaders play an essential role in confirming whether the prophetic word aligns with the doctrine of the church and the vision for the body. This safeguard creates a healthy prophetic culture, where accountability and submission are seen as strengths, not weaknesses. It also strengthens the trust between the prophetic ministry and leadership, creating unity in the church as God's will is revealed.

Creating a Culture That Embraces Healthy Prophetic Ministry

To cultivate a healthy prophetic culture, a church must create an environment where prophecy is both welcomed and respected. This begins with leaders who set the example, openly valuing the prophetic and encouraging its practice in a safe and controlled manner.

Leaders must teach their congregations about the role of prophecy, the nature of hearing God's voice, and the importance of humility in delivering prophetic words. A healthy prophetic culture also involves training and equipping the body of Christ to hear God for themselves.

When believers understand their own capacity to hear God's voice, the prophetic ministry becomes not just a few "special people" in the church, but a movement that includes all who are willing to listen and respond. Training should involve teaching the congregation how to test prophetic words, how to distinguish between God's voice and other voices, and how to receive and respond to prophecy in a way that honors God and edifies the church.

Moreover, a healthy prophetic culture avoids sensationalism and extremes. Prophecy should never be used to manipulate, control, or cause division. Instead, it should build up the church, bring clarity to the direction of the body, and confirm what God is already doing.

When prophecy is approached with reverence, respect, and the fear of the Lord, it can flow freely and powerfully, bringing transformation to the lives of individuals and to the entire congregation. Building this culture takes time and intentional effort.

Leaders need to actively create opportunities for prophetic ministry to be practiced and tested. This might include prophetic workshops, group activations, or moments during services where individuals can share prophetic words under the oversight of leaders.

As this culture grows, the church will see an increasing number of believers stepping out in faith, bringing words of life, healing, and encouragement that impact not just the church, but also the community around them. When the prophetic is done right, it becomes a catalyst for personal and corporate revival.

Fostering an Atmosphere of Safety and Growth

One of the greatest challenges in developing a healthy prophetic culture is ensuring that the prophetic remains a safe space for both the individual delivering the word and the church body receiving it. There will always be a risk of getting it wrong, but that should not stop anyone from stepping out in faith.

Prophets, like anyone learning a new skill, must be given

room to grow, make mistakes, and learn from them. When a prophetic word does not hit the mark, the church leadership should provide grace, offering correction and encouragement in a way that builds up the individual and protects the integrity of the ministry.

This environment of safety is essential for the development of mature prophetic voices. It encourages believers to take risks, stretch their faith, and step into new realms of revelation. As the prophetic ministry grows, the prophetic voices in the church will become more finely tuned to God's heart, bringing greater clarity and precision.

Additionally, the church as a whole will grow in its understanding of prophecy, making it a regular and cherished part of the church culture. In a healthy prophetic environment, there is room for both celebration and correction, as both are needed for growth.

When prophetic words align with God's heart and purpose, they become a testament to His faithfulness and goodness. These words act as a guide, pointing the church towards the fulfillment of God's plans. And as the prophetic ministry matures, the entire church body benefits from the strength, clarity, and unity that prophetic revelation brings.

Prophetic ministry is a beautiful gift from God, but it must be practiced with wisdom, humility, and order within the local church. By understanding the role of prophecy in corporate worship, submitting prophetic words to leadership, and fostering a healthy prophetic culture, we ensure that the prophetic remains a vital and powerful tool for building up the body of Christ.

Prophecy, when done correctly, has the ability to bring clarity, encouragement, and direction to the Church, empowering believers to walk in God's will and fulfill their purpose on the earth. Let us embrace this ministry with reverence and intentionality, always seeking to glorify God and serve His people with the words He gives us.

Reflection Questions

1. How can you ensure that the prophetic words you share in a church setting align with the vision and direction of the leadership while remaining faithful to God's voice?
2. In what ways can your church create an atmosphere that values both the freedom to prophesy and the accountability needed to maintain order and spiritual health?

Activations

1. **Practice Submission:** This week, ask your church leadership for permission to share a prophetic word you believe God has given you. Invite their feedback and be open to their discernment, using the experience to grow in humility and alignment with church protocol.
2. **Cultivate a Healthy Culture:** Partner with a group of believers to practice hearing God's voice in a safe environment, such as a small group or workshop. Focus on delivering encouraging and edifying words while receiving feedback, creating a space for growth and mutual accountability.

CHAPTER 10
GROWING IN PROPHETIC BOLDNESS

Prophecy is a vital and empowering gift, but one of the greatest hurdles many face in the prophetic journey is the fear of stepping out. Whether it's the fear of making mistakes, being judged, or simply not feeling "spiritual enough," these obstacles can often silence the prophetic voice that God wants to speak through you.

But the truth is, boldness is a key ingredient in fulfilling the calling of every believer to prophesy. God desires for His people to operate in prophetic boldness, speaking His heart with confidence and clarity.

Overcoming the Fear of Stepping Out

Fear is one of the greatest barriers to walking in the fullness of the prophetic. Many believers know in their hearts that God is speaking to them, but when it comes time to share what they've received, they hesitate. The fear of rejection, misinterpretation, or the pressure to be "accurate" can paralyze the prophetic gift. But it is essential to recognize that boldness does not mean perfection

—it means trust. Boldness is the willingness to step out in faith, knowing that God is with you, regardless of the outcome. Let me share a personal story with you to paint the picture.

I remember a specific moment when I was in a church service, and I felt God prompting me to share a word with someone. My heart raced, and I struggled with doubt, wondering if it was truly from God. But I knew I had to act. I'd had the Lord speak to me, the name Sarah and I had a lady highlighted, but I've never met her before.

When I finally approached her, I asked her who Sarah was. She said Sarah is my sister. and I asked her what was going on that week with Sarah? She said wow I haven't seen my sister in years and I'm really nervous because this week we go on a weeklong road trip across the country together. It turned out she had been struggling with anxiety about the trip and my word provided the encouragement and peace she needed. That moment was a turning point for me, realizing that boldness isn't about getting it perfect but about trusting God to speak through me.

It's important to understand that prophecy is not about the person delivering the word, but about God's heart being communicated to His people. Your role is simply to be a vessel. God can use anyone who is willing to step out in obedience. He's not looking for flawless execution, but for hearts that are willing to partner with His Holy Spirit. As you step out, you may stumble or feel uncertain at times, but with each step, you grow in boldness, and the voice of God becomes clearer in your life.

Building Confidence Through Practice

The only way to overcome fear and gain prophetic boldness is through practice. Prophesy is a skill, and like any skill, it improves the more you use it. The process of stepping out and releasing prophetic words requires practice and experience. As you begin to take risks, the fear that once gripped you begins to lose its hold. Each prophetic word you release builds your confidence, and you begin to understand the rhythm of hearing God and delivering His message with clarity.

I started with a guy at church who was at the alter for prayer, my pastor had asked me to help pray for people. I wasn't trained and I didn't know, to ask what he wanted prayer for. I shared with him what I saw, I gave him a word about an upcoming job opportunity I saw the Lord bringing his way. It felt so simple, but he shared that the word confirmed something they had been praying about for weeks, and the lady next to him (I found out later was his wife) said in an excited voice oh my God, honey I told you. That experience showed me how practicing the prophetic in safe spaces gave me the courage to speak out more often.

Start small. Prophetic words don't always need to be grand declarations for large groups. Begin by sharing simple words of encouragement with individuals—whether it's a word of comfort, insight, or direction. As you see the impact that these simple words can have, you'll realize that God is using you in ways you didn't expect. Confidence grows through small steps of obedience, which gradually lead to more significant prophetic moments.

Testimonies of Lives Changed Through Simple Prophetic Words

One of the most powerful ways to grow in boldness is by

seeing the transformation that simple prophetic words can bring. God's heart is always to bring encouragement, healing, and direction through prophecy. Prophetic words are not meant to be heavy or condemning but rather vessels of His love and truth.

The beauty of prophecy is that it can change lives in the most unexpected ways, and when you witness the fruit of your obedience, it ignites a deeper passion to continue prophesying. There are countless stories of individuals whose lives were radically changed by a prophetic word spoken at just the right moment. Perhaps it was a word of encouragement when someone was ready to give up, or a prophetic insight that brought clarity in a season of confusion.

Sometimes, the words are simple—a reminder that God sees them, or an affirmation of something God had already been speaking to their hearts. Yet, these simple words often carry profound impact, both for the receiver and for the one delivering the word. The more you step out in boldness, the more you will see the transforming power of prophecy in action.

Stepping Into Prophetic Boldness: A Lifelong Journey

Growing in prophetic boldness is not a one-time event but a lifelong journey. It's a process of continually stepping out in faith, learning to trust God more deeply, and allowing His voice to guide you with greater clarity. Every time you say "yes" to God's call, you deepen your relationship with Him and increase your capacity to hear His voice and speak His heart.

In one particular season of life, I felt completely unequipped to step into the prophetic in a larger way. I wasn't sure I was hearing God clearly. But as I kept saying 'yes,' I noticed my prophetic gift growing. Looking back, I can see how those initial moments of doubt turned into foundational experiences that shaped my prophetic boldness today. God was faithful to use me, even when I didn't feel ready.

Don't let fear or past mistakes hold you back. Prophetic boldness is nurtured through humility, willingness, and obedience. As you mature in the prophetic, you'll notice that your boldness becomes a natural expression of your relationship with God. It's no longer about striving to get it right, but about flowing with His Spirit, speaking what He is saying, and trusting that He will accomplish His purposes through you.

God is raising up a generation of prophetic voices who are not afraid to speak boldly and clearly into the lives of others. As you grow in your prophetic gift, know that you are part of something bigger than yourself—a movement of believers who are declaring God's heart, bringing hope, healing, and transformation wherever they go. Each word you speak in faith has the potential to bring about divine change. So, step out with boldness, knowing that as you speak God's heart, you are fulfilling your purpose as His mouthpiece to the world.

Prophetic boldness is a key element in fulfilling God's call on your life. It requires overcoming fear, practicing regularly, and recognizing the power of simple words to change lives. As you grow in confidence, remember that prophecy is about God's love being made manifest in the world, and your willingness to be used by Him is what truly matters. So, take that step today. Let your voice be one that declares God's heart, bringing life and hope wherever you go.

Reflection Questions

1. What fears or hesitations have kept you from stepping out in prophetic boldness, and how can you address those fears with faith and trust in God?
2. Reflect on a time when a simple act of obedience led to a positive outcome for someone else. How did that experience shape your confidence in hearing and speaking God's voice?

Activations

1. Ask God to highlight someone in your life who needs encouragement. Write down what you feel God is saying about them, then boldly share it with them in a loving and humble way.
2. Spend 10 minutes in prayer, asking the Holy Spirit to show you an area where He wants you to grow in boldness. Declare aloud that you will overcome fear and step out in faith to deliver prophetic words as He leads.

CHAPTER 11
ACTIVATING THE GIFT OF PROPHECY

The gift of prophecy is one that must be activated in the life of every believer. Prophecy is not something that operates only through a select few but is a tool meant for the entire body of Christ. Activation is the process of stepping into this gift by faith, allowing the Holy Spirit to flow through you, and learning to listen and respond to God's voice in real-time. As we grow in the prophetic, we learn to steward this powerful gift and use it to encourage and edify others.

How to Begin Prophesying: Practical Exercises and Activations

For many believers, stepping into prophecy can feel intimidating. However, like any spiritual gift, prophecy grows stronger through practice and obedience. The first step in activating the prophetic gift is to simply take a step of faith, trusting that God desires to speak through you. Prophecy isn't reserved for a select few; it's for every believer, and it is meant to edify, encourage, and comfort. Here are several practical exercises to help you begin prophesying and activate the gift within you:

1. **START WITH SCRIPTURE:** One of the simplest ways to begin activating prophecy is by speaking life into the promises of God found in the Bible. Scripture is rich with divine truths, and these promises are often directly relevant to the lives of those around us.

To begin, spend time reading a passage of scripture and ask God to show you a specific word to share with someone based on that passage. For instance, you might read Isaiah 41:10: "Fear not, for I am with you; be not dismayed, for I am your God," and feel prompted to share this with someone facing a difficult situation. By speaking God's Word over others, you're stepping into the prophetic role of speaking life into circumstances.

The Word of God carries power, and as you speak it, you are releasing God's heart for the person or situation at hand. You can also practice looking for God's character revealed through Scripture. For example, when reading a Psalm or a passage about Jesus' nature, ask God to reveal to you a deeper truth or promise for someone you know. As you engage in this practice, you will see how God begins to illuminate His Word in a fresh way, strengthening your ability to discern His heart.

2. **ACTIVATE THROUGH PRAYER:** Prayer is a gateway for prophetic activation. As you pray for others, you begin to align your heart with God's desires for their lives. While praying, take time to listen for the still small voice of God. The Holy Spirit speaks in many ways—through impressions, visions, thoughts, or even a knowing in your spirit. As you feel prompted, speak out the words God is impressing on your heart. Even if the words seem simple, they can be deeply prophetic when they are led by the Spirit.

For example, you might be praying for a friend who is

struggling with anxiety and suddenly sense the word "peace" in your spirit. You can then declare, "I speak peace over you right now in the name of Jesus." This simple prophetic act, though small, can break chains and bring peace into that person's life. Practicing this type of prayer regularly will help you recognize when the Holy Spirit is prompting you to speak with prophetic insight.

3. Practice Listening to God's Voice: Taking time to simply listen to God is one of the most important practices in growing in prophecy. Find a quiet place, free from distractions, where you can tune your heart to the Lord. Set aside time to ask God to speak to you, and then patiently listen for His voice. It can be helpful to ask specific questions, such as, "God, do you have a word for someone I know?" or "Lord, what do you want to say to me today?"

As you listen, be aware that prophetic words don't always have to be grand or dramatic. Often, God speaks in quiet, gentle whispers or through brief impressions. A simple Bible verse, an encouraging word, or a prophetic image can be a message from the Lord. Once you sense that God has spoken, share what you've received with others, even if it feels small or insignificant. The act of speaking out the word in faith will strengthen your prophetic muscles and make it easier for you to discern God's voice in the future.

4. Journal Your Prophetic Words: Writing down the words you receive from God is a powerful way to increase your sensitivity to His voice. When you hear from God, whether it's for yourself or someone else, record it in a journal. This practice will help you discern patterns, recognize the voice of God more clearly, and increase your faith as you look back and see how accurate and timely your prophetic words have been.

In your journal, include any impressions, Bible verses, dreams, or visions that you receive. As you continue journaling, you will begin to notice trends in the types of words or themes God tends to speak to you. You may find that God frequently speaks to you about hope, healing, or restoration, for example. This understanding will not only increase your confidence but will also deepen your relationship with God as you see His voice consistently guiding you.

5. PARTICIPATE IN GROUP ACTIVATIONS: One of the best ways to practice prophecy is within the context of community. Gather with a group of like-minded believers, and create opportunities for each person to activate the prophetic gift. You can do this by taking turns sharing what you believe God is saying for someone in the group. It's important to maintain a safe and encouraging environment, where everyone is free to step out without fear of judgment.

A simple exercise could involve one person sharing a brief, personal story or prayer request, while others listen and then share what they feel God might be saying to that person. As you step out in faith together, you'll not only grow in your prophetic abilities but will also strengthen the body of Christ by speaking life into one another's lives. The more you practice this, the more natural it will feel, and the clearer God's voice will become.

6. STAY HUMBLE AND TEACHABLE: As you begin to prophesy, it's crucial to remain humble and teachable. Prophecy is a gift, and as with any gift, it's important to remember that you are a vessel, not the source. Always approach prophecy with a heart of humility, recognizing that you're an instrument through which God speaks, and not someone who "owns" the gift.

If you make a mistake, don't be discouraged. Prophetic ministry is a learning process, and every believer's journey is unique. God is gracious and will help you refine your ability to hear Him more clearly. Stay open to correction and feedback from trusted leaders or fellow believers, and allow God to continue to shape and mold your prophetic gift over time.

As you practice these activations with a humble heart, you will grow in your ability to hear and speak God's heart with increasing clarity and confidence. By regularly practicing these exercises, you will be taking intentional steps toward activating the prophetic gift within you. As you continue to step out in faith, you will see God's voice become clearer, and His words will become more powerful and life-giving to those around you.

Remember, prophecy is not just about speaking; it's about being a vessel through which God speaks into the lives of others, bringing His love, encouragement, and guidance to the world. I remember the first time I activated the gift of prophecy on demand so to speak. There was a group of Pastors in West Africa and one by one we began to prophecy over them, and as we did, the atmosphere opened more and more to where you could see deeper and deeper into their lives, and the words became super specific and crazy accurate.

The words we shared—deeply resonated with them and provided the clarity they had been seeking. That moment showed me that prophecy doesn't have to be complicated; it's about speaking what God places on your heart.

Group Activations for Churches and Small Groups

One of the most effective environments for activating the

prophetic gift is within the context of a community of believers. When we gather in smaller groups, whether in a church setting or in a home group, we create a safe space for learning, practicing, and growing in the prophetic. Group activations provide opportunities for believers to step out in faith, receive feedback, and refine their ability to hear and respond to God's voice.

These activations help build a supportive environment where individuals can grow together, gain confidence, and encourage one another in their prophetic journeys. Here are several group activation exercises that can help foster prophetic growth in a church or small group setting:

> *1. Prophetic Sharing Circles:* One of the simplest yet most effective group activations is the "Prophetic Sharing Circle." In this exercise, everyone gathers in a circle, and each person asks God for a prophetic word for the person sitting to their left. It's important to create a relaxed and open environment where individuals feel safe to share, even if they are unsure of what they are hearing.
>
> The key is to encourage the group to trust in the Holy Spirit's guidance and to speak in faith, even if the words feel simple or small. For example, someone might ask God for a word for their neighbor in the circle and receive a thought like, "You are a beacon of light in your workplace." This word may be given with the full confidence that it will resonate with the person it's spoken to, even if it seems like a general encouragement.
>
> After each person shares their word, the group can take a moment for feedback. The individual who received the word may affirm how it applies to their life, or they

can ask for clarification if the word doesn't quite resonate with them. This activity is great for building trust and encouraging the group. It helps participants become comfortable with listening to God's voice and sharing what they hear in a safe, supportive environment.

Additionally, receiving feedback allows individuals to refine their prophetic gifting by learning to discern when they are hearing God's voice clearly and how to deliver it in a way that encourages others. This can be especially helpful for new prophetic believers who are just beginning to step out in faith.

2. *Word for the Nation or City:* Another powerful group activation exercise is to ask God for a prophetic word for a broader context, such as a city, church, or nation. This helps participants step out of their personal context and learn to hear God for the bigger picture. As you gather as a group, create a moment where everyone focuses on asking the Holy Spirit to reveal something significant for your city, church, or nation.

Take turns sharing what you hear, whether it's a scripture, an impression, a vision, or a specific word. For instance, a participant may hear a word like, "I see a revival fire beginning to spread through our city," or, "God is calling this church to be a place of refuge and healing for the brokenhearted." These words can be deeply prophetic and impactful for the group, as they give direction and vision for the collective body.

Once everyone has shared, pray over the words that have been given, trusting that God is speaking through each person to bring clarity and direction. This is also a great way to discern the unity of the Spirit, as multiple people may receive similar themes or images, affirming that God is speaking to the group as a whole.

Praying over the prophetic words for the city or church also creates an opportunity to intercede for the place or people being prophesied over. It allows the group to partner with God in His plans for the future, releasing prayer and prophetic declarations that align with God's will. This exercise not only strengthens individual prophetic gifting but also encourages group unity and alignment with God's heart for a larger purpose.

3. Treasure Hunts: One of the most exciting and adventurous prophetic activation exercises is the "Treasure Hunt." This exercise, which has been popularized by prophetic ministries, involves asking God to reveal a specific person, location, or need that He wants you to speak into. The idea is to "hunt" for the "treasure" God shows you, whether it's a specific individual, a situation, or a place.

You can carry out this activity in pairs or small groups, and it's often done in a public setting such as a park, a mall, or a busy street. For example, before heading out, the group may pray and ask God to reveal details such as a person's appearance, their current need, or a specific location where God wants to minister to someone. One person might get a word like, "Look for a man wearing a red hat who is struggling with back pain." The group then goes out, actively looking for the person who fits the description. Once they find them, they can engage the individual, sharing the prophetic word, praying for them, and ministering in the power of the Holy Spirit.

The Treasure Hunt exercise builds both prophetic sensitivity and boldness. As participants learn to listen for specific details, they grow in their ability to discern God's voice in everyday situations. It also stretches believers to step out of their comfort zones, practicing the prophetic in real-world contexts and learning to speak God's truth to strangers. In addition to activating prophetic gifts, this exercise often leads to powerful moments of healing, encouragement, and evangelism, as God uses the prophetic to touch lives in a tangible way.

4. Personal Testimony Spot: Reflecting on personal testimony is a key component of prophetic activation because it helps believers see how God has worked in their own lives through prophetic ministry. Before or after participating in a group activation like a prophetic circle or Treasure Hunt, take time to reflect and share personal testimonies of how prophetic words have impacted your life.

This exercise not only strengthens individual faith but also builds the faith of the entire group, as they hear how God has been faithful in speaking and answering prophetic prayers. For example, someone might share a story of how, during a prophetic circle, they received a word of encouragement at a difficult time in their life, and how that word became a turning point in their journey.

Another person might share how a prophetic word

spoken to them during a Treasure Hunt led to a powerful healing or opened doors for ministry opportunities. These testimonies encourage the group to keep stepping out in faith, knowing that God is using their prophetic words to bring real transformation. In addition to encouraging faith, personal testimonies help clarify how to deliver prophetic words with love, humility, and accuracy.

The more we practice sharing testimonies of God's goodness and faithfulness, the more we strengthen our understanding of how prophetic words should align with God's heart, promoting healing, restoration, and encouragement in others. By engaging in these group activations, believers will grow not only in their ability to hear God's voice but also in their confidence to step out and speak His words with boldness.

Group activations provide a safe and supportive environment where individuals can learn, grow, and refine their prophetic gifting, all while strengthening the body of Christ and working together to release God's heart into the world.

I remember being part of a treasure hunt activity where the group was sent out to find people we felt God had highlighted. I had a strong sense that God wanted me to speak to a woman I passed on the street. I hesitated at first, but when I stepped out, she began to cry, saying that she had been praying for a sign from God. It reminded me of how powerful it can be when we step out together, and how God uses our obedience to reveal His heart.

Staying Humble and Teachable

As we grow in our prophetic gift, it is essential to remain humble and teachable. The prophetic journey is one of learning and refining. Even the most seasoned prophetic voices must stay open to correction, growth, and development. Humility allows us to continually yield to the Holy Spirit and avoid becoming prideful or self-reliant in our gifting.

1. **Receive Feedback:** Just as with any skill, prophetic ministry requires feedback from others. Don't be afraid to ask trusted leaders or friends for input on the words you deliver. This helps refine your prophetic sensitivity and ensures you're aligned with God's heart.

2. **Be Open to God's Timing:** Sometimes, the prophetic word doesn't come immediately or it may require a season of waiting. Don't rush the process. Humility means submitting to God's timing and trusting that He will speak when He is ready.

3. **Avoid Comparing:** It can be easy to compare your prophetic journey to others, but remember that God uses each person uniquely. Your gifting may look different from someone else's, and that's okay. Stay focused on what God is doing in your life and the call He's placed on you.

4. **Cultivate a Lifestyle of Prayer:** A teachable spirit is nurtured through a consistent prayer life. The more time you spend in God's presence, the more sensitive you become to His voice. A life of prayer is essential to hearing and activating the prophetic.

Stepping Into the Prophetic Flow

Activating the gift of prophecy is an exciting and rewarding journey. It begins with simple steps of faith and grows through practice and obedience. As you engage in prophetic exercises and remain humble and teachable, the Holy Spirit will increasingly flow through you. The key is to stay faithful to the process, embrace opportunities for activation, and continually seek to hear God's voice with clarity.

You were created to hear from God and to speak His heart to others. As you step into this prophetic flow, you will become a vessel through which God can communicate His love, direction, and encouragement to the world around you. Let your prophetic journey begin today—one step, one word, at a time.

Reflection Questions

1. How has your understanding of prophecy as a gift for all believers challenged or encouraged you in your faith journey?
2. What obstacles have held you back from stepping out in prophetic activation, and how can you partner with the Holy Spirit to overcome them?

Activations

1. **Personal Scripture Activation:** Spend 10 minutes reading a passage of Scripture, asking God to highlight a specific verse or promise. Write down what He reveals, and share it with a friend or family member, explaining why you feel it applies to them.
2. **Listening Prayer Exercise:** Set aside 15 minutes in a quiet space. Ask God to give you a prophetic word or encouragement for someone you know. Write down what you sense, and prayerfully share it with that person, trusting God to speak through you.

CHAPTER 12
PROPHETIC LIFESTYLE

The prophetic gift is not just a function of ministry; it is a lifestyle—a way of living in constant awareness of God's presence and a heart to speak His will and heart into every situation. As believers, we are called not only to operate in prophetic moments but to embody a prophetic lifestyle, where hearing God's voice and speaking His heart becomes natural and integral to our daily lives.

Prophecy as Part of Your Everyday Life

Living a prophetic lifestyle means that prophecy flows naturally from the intimate relationship we cultivate with God. Prophetic words are not just for church meetings or ministry settings—they are meant to be spoken in every area of life. In your home, workplace, and community, you are called to be a voice of hope, life, and encouragement, bringing the heart of God into the practical situations of everyday life.

The apostle Paul encouraged believers to earnestly desire spiritual gifts, especially prophecy (1 Corinthians 14:1), and that desire should not be confined to a specific moment or location.

Instead, prophecy should permeate all that we do. When we walk into a room, we should be so attuned to God that we are ready to speak His heart, offering life and direction to those around us. We are His representatives, and through prophecy, we demonstrate the love, hope, and power of God in action.

For example, you might be in a grocery store, and as you interact with the cashier, you sense that they are struggling with loneliness. Instead of just offering a polite "Have a good day," you might take a moment to speak encouragement, telling them that God sees their heart and that He is with them in their struggles. This may be a simple word, but it can deeply impact someone's life, showing them that God is near, speaking directly to their heart.

Seeing People Through God's Eyes

A prophetic lifestyle begins with seeing people as God sees them. Often, we are quick to judge based on outward appearances or our own assumptions, but a prophetic heart is one that sees beneath the surface, recognizing the potential and destiny in others. The prophetic allows us to look past the external struggles, flaws, or failures of individuals and speak into their God-given purpose.

When we begin to see people the way God sees them, we will begin to speak life into their identity rather than reinforcing their insecurities. This is a key component of the prophetic lifestyle: it's not just about receiving a word and delivering it—it's about cultivating a mindset of love and compassion that naturally sees people through the eyes of a loving Father.

For instance, when interacting with a colleague who may

seem difficult or frustrated, instead of viewing them as an obstacle, you can ask God to show you their heart. Perhaps He reveals a deep desire for success and validation. With this insight, you can speak encouragement, affirming their worth and potential, letting them know that God has a plan for their success. This approach demonstrates the power of prophecy in everyday life—not as something distant or abstract, but as a tangible expression of God's love and vision for people.

Speaking Life and Hope Wherever You Go

A prophetic lifestyle is marked by a constant release of life and hope. As you go about your day, the words you speak carry the potential to either build up or tear down. As prophetic believers, we are called to speak life into every conversation, every interaction, and every situation. Jesus Himself was the perfect example of a prophetic life.

He didn't just deliver words of prophecy in special moments—He spoke life wherever He went. He addressed the brokenhearted, gave hope to the hopeless, and proclaimed freedom to the captives. Similarly, our prophetic lifestyle should embody these same principles. Everywhere we go, we should be ready to declare God's promises, speak healing, and encourage others to live according to their divine destiny.

Take, for example, a conversation with a friend who is facing a difficult situation, such as a job loss or family crisis. Rather than offering just sympathy or advice, the prophetic believer will ask God for a word of encouragement and direction. Maybe God reveals to you that your friend is about to step into a season of new opportunities, or that He has already begun to work on their behalf in unseen ways. These prophetic words of hope bring a new perspective and perspective shift that can empower your friend to press forward in faith.

Cultivating a Prophetic Lifestyle of Discernment and Wisdom

A prophetic lifestyle is also one that is cultivated with discernment and wisdom. It's important to understand that prophecy is not just about speaking when prompted—it's about knowing how and when to speak. In any situation, we must be sensitive to the Holy Spirit's timing, ensuring that the words we speak align with God's purpose and bring forth the desired result.

This level of discernment comes through intimacy with the Holy Spirit, through listening attentively to His voice, and understanding that not every moment is the right time to release a prophetic word. Sometimes, the prophetic word is meant to be prayed into or held for a later time, and wisdom is needed to know when to speak and when to wait. For instance, in a tense or emotional situation, it may not always be the right time to release a word.

The person you are ministering to may not yet be ready to receive it, or the Holy Spirit may be leading you to pray silently over the situation first. Cultivating this sensitivity and discerning God's timing and method is essential in living a prophetic lifestyle that is both impactful and respectful.

A Prophetic Lifestyle of Love, Life, and Purpose

Ultimately, living a prophetic lifestyle is about more than simply delivering prophetic words—it's about embodying the heart of God in everything we do. It's about being vessels that carry His life, hope, and purpose into every corner of the world. Whether at work, at home, or in casual encounters, we are called to be the mouthpiece of God, speaking words of life and encouragement that draw people closer to Him.

A prophetic lifestyle is marked by a consistent release of God's heart, by seeing others through His eyes, and by being intentional with the words we speak. As we live out this prophetic lifestyle, we fulfill our calling to be God's ambassadors on earth, bringing His kingdom into every sphere of influence. It is not just an occasional ministry—it's a way of life. It's about making God's voice and His heart accessible to those around us, everywhere we go. Let your prophetic lifestyle shine brightly, speaking life and bringing hope to a world in desperate need of God's touch.

Reflection Questions

1. How can you cultivate greater intimacy with God so that hearing His voice and speaking His heart becomes natural in your daily life?
2. In what areas of your life—home, work, or community—can you intentionally begin to see people through God's eyes and speak life into their identity?

Activations

1. **Prophetic Encouragement in Action:** This week, intentionally ask God for a prophetic word of encouragement for someone you encounter (e.g., a coworker, friend, or stranger). Speak the word with love, sensitivity, and wisdom, trusting that it will bring hope and life. Reflect on the outcome and what you learned from the experience.
2. **Seeing Through God's Eyes Exercise:** Spend 15 minutes in prayer, asking God to show you how He sees a specific person you may find challenging or difficult to understand. Write down any insights or impressions He gives you. Use this perspective to pray for them and, if possible, speak life and encouragement to them.

CHAPTER 13
THE FUTURE OF PROPHETIC MINISTRY

As we approach the future of prophetic ministry, we must recognize that the prophetic gift is not just a static function within the church; it is a dynamic, ever-expanding force meant to influence every aspect of society. It's a ministry that is designed to go beyond the walls of the church and penetrate the very fabric of everyday life.

We are entering an age where prophetic voices will rise with increasing clarity, authority, and urgency, leading God's people to fulfill their divine assignments—especially in the crucial days ahead. The role of prophecy in the end-time church is more pivotal than ever. The scriptures speak of a great outpouring of the Spirit in the last days:

"And it shall come to pass in the last days, says God, that I will pour out my Spirit on all flesh, and your sons and your daughters shall prophesy, your young men shall see visions, your old men shall dream dreams" (Acts 2:17) NKJV

This is not just a select few within the body of Christ who

will prophesy—it is an outpouring that touches all of God's people. In these last days, prophecy will be central in guiding the church through the challenges and uncertainties that will come. The prophetic will not only direct the Church toward God's heart but will also provide direction for the nations.

We must also understand that the prophetic gift is not isolated to church buildings or ministry gatherings. While the Church is a place for prophetic activity, the world outside the church is in desperate need of the voice of God. Prophetic believers are being raised up in every sphere of influence: in the marketplace, education, government, arts, and media.

Prophecy is going beyond the four walls of the church and is being strategically placed in the hands of believers to impact and transform industries, governments, schools, families, and communities. The prophetic will no longer be confined to individuals in ministry roles; it will be a tool for revival and transformation in every area of life.

This next phase of prophetic ministry will involve a greater integration between the prophetic and the practical. God's people will not only receive prophetic words that comfort, exhort, and edify, but they will also begin to speak prophetic truth into areas that have remained untouched by God's influence for too long.

The prophetic will be instrumental in discerning strategies for societal transformation, bringing light into the darkness and direction to those who have lost their way. This will require prophetic voices to be both spiritually attuned and practically engaged in shaping the culture. The Church, as God's prophetic people, will be tasked with influencing all areas of life, equipping believers to prophesy not only in church settings but also in the workplace, in their homes, and in public spaces. Raising up prophetic believers in every sphere of influence is a powerful vision for the future of prophetic ministry.

God is positioning His prophetic people in strategic areas where their influence will be felt deeply. The marketplace is one such arena where prophetic voices will rise, bringing divine solutions to business, leadership, and economic problems. In the world of politics, government officials will need prophetic insight to navigate the complex issues they face.

Artists, musicians, and media influencers will speak prophetic words that reshape culture and awaken the hearts of those in their spheres. Educators will be empowered to speak life into young people and bring heaven's perspective into the classroom. The future of prophetic ministry is not just for the pulpit but for every believer to step into their unique calling, bringing the power of God's word to influence their world.

To step into this greater calling, we must press into greater intimacy with God. The key to walking in the fullness of prophetic ministry in this new era is intimacy with the Holy Spirit. It is in the place of deep communion with God that we will hear His voice clearly and understand His heart for the people around us. As we grow in our relationship with God, we will not only receive prophetic words for others but will also learn how to carry His heart of love and compassion for those we minister to.

The prophetic is about speaking the heart of God, not just delivering a message. It's about becoming His mouthpiece, bringing hope, healing, and restoration wherever we go. Equipping a prophetic generation is not just about imparting the gift of prophecy—it's about equipping a generation to carry the burden of the Lord. Prophetic ministry is not just for those with a specific calling; it is for every believer.

As we move forward, the church must cultivate a culture of prophecy, encouraging and empowering every member to step into their prophetic calling. This involves not only training but also creating environments where people can practice hearing God's voice and stepping out in faith. This kind of equipping requires a shift in our mindset—recognizing that the prophetic is not just for the spiritually elite but for all believers who are willing to listen and obey God's voice.

Faith and perseverance will be required for prophetic believers in the days ahead. The journey of growing in prophetic ministry will not always be easy. There will be times of testing, times when we get it wrong, and times when we face opposition. But God is calling us to press forward in faith, knowing that He is refining our hearts and increasing our capacity to carry His word. As we continue to seek His voice, we will grow in confidence, clarity, and boldness, knowing that the power of the prophetic is greater than any challenge we might face.

We must trust that God is faithful to complete the good work He has begun in us, and He will use us as vessels of His will in the earth. As we enter this next era of prophetic ministry, we must be bold in stepping out. God is calling His people to speak His truth, to declare His promises, and to speak life into the world around them.

Prophecy is not just a gift we receive but a gift we steward, a gift that must be released for the benefit of the Church and the world. The prophetic will continue to play a vital role in shaping the future, directing the course of nations, and ushering in the Kingdom of God. We must continue to press in, step out, and speak forth what God is revealing in this season.

The future of prophetic ministry is bright and full of possibility. It will not be limited to a select few but will be released through the body of Christ, empowering believers to bring God's kingdom to earth. The world is in desperate need of God's voice, and we, as His prophetic people, must rise up, speak His truth, and bring His hope to the nations.

The best days of the prophetic ministry are ahead of us. Keep pressing in, stay faithful to the call, and continue to release God's heart wherever you go. The world is waiting for the voice of God to speak through His people, and the time to rise up and fulfill our prophetic destiny is now.

Reflection Questions

1. **Personal Calling:** In what ways do you sense God calling you to be a prophetic voice in your sphere of influence? How can you begin or continue to step into that calling?
2. **Intimacy with God:** How does your relationship with the Holy Spirit impact your ability to hear and speak God's heart? What steps can you take to deepen that intimacy?

Activations

1. **Prophetic Outreach:** Ask God to reveal someone in your workplace, community, or family who needs to hear His heart. Spend time in prayer, listen for a word of encouragement or insight, and share it with that person in love.
2. **Strategic Intercession:** Choose a specific sphere of influence (e.g., education, government, arts, business) and spend time praying for prophetic voices to rise in that area. Ask God for a prophetic strategy or word that could bring transformation, and write it down to declare in prayer.

CONCLUSION
EMPOWERED TO PROPHESY

As we come to the close of this book, we find ourselves standing at the threshold of a new season for the body of Christ. The prophetic gift is not just for the few—it is for every believer, and God is stirring His Church to step into a greater manifestation of His voice in the world. Through the principles we've explored in this book, you've been equipped to hear God's voice more clearly, respond to His promptings with boldness, and speak His heart with love and honor.

You've learned that prophecy is not a mystical, unreachable gift reserved for only the most spiritually advanced. It is a tool given to every believer to encourage, build up, and direct others toward God's purposes. The purpose of prophecy is rooted in love—it is an expression of God's care for His people, designed to reveal His heart, His plans, and His will for individuals, families, communities, and nations. You are empowered to prophesy, not as a mere bystander but as a partner with the Holy Spirit in His work on the earth.

At its core, the prophetic is about partnership with God. It's about knowing His heart and speaking it out with clarity and confidence, whether you're sharing a word in the local church or bringing light to someone in your everyday life. The prophetic flows from the deep well of intimacy with God—He desires to speak to each of us, and He is speaking.

The question is not whether God is speaking, but whether we are listening and responding. In each chapter, we've emphasized the importance of alignment with Scripture, the need for sensitivity to the Holy Spirit, and the requirement of love and humility in prophetic ministry. All these elements work together to create a prophetic culture that is healthy, effective, and transformational.

When we prophesy out of love and in obedience to God, we become His mouthpiece on earth. This responsibility is not a light one, but it is an incredible privilege. As you move forward, step out in faith. The more you practice hearing God's voice and delivering prophetic words, the more natural it will become. You'll experience firsthand the power of a prophetic word to bring breakthrough, comfort, healing, and direction to those around you.

Remember, prophecy isn't just about grand declarations—sometimes it's the simple, everyday words of encouragement that hold the greatest power. God will use you in ways you never imagined to speak life to those who need it most. The journey you've begun is not one of perfection but one of growth. The prophetic is a continual process of learning, testing, and refining. Don't be discouraged if you make mistakes or feel unsure at times.

This is all part of the journey. The more you grow in intimacy with God, the more confident you will become in hearing

His voice and speaking His word. It's a journey of faith, trust, and obedience, and as you walk in that faith, God will meet you every step of the way.

The future of prophetic ministry is bright, and God is raising up a generation of prophetic believers who will impact every area of society. The prophetic voice is not limited to the church—it is needed in every sphere of influence. Whether in the workplace, the arts, education, politics, or family life, prophetic believers are called to speak God's truth, release His wisdom, and bring His presence wherever they go.

The Church's prophetic destiny is not confined to its gatherings; it is meant to permeate every corner of the earth, transforming culture and advancing the Kingdom of God. Now is the time to step into your calling as a prophetic believer. As you begin to exercise the gift of prophecy, be encouraged that your voice is powerful. You are God's mouthpiece, and the words you speak can shape destinies, release healing, and bring clarity to those who are in need of His guidance.

Whether you are called to prophesy over individuals or speak to entire nations, your obedience to His voice is crucial in this hour. Let the prophetic become a part of your everyday lifestyle. See those around you through God's eyes, and speak life into every situation. Allow the Holy Spirit to use you to prophesy in the marketplace, in your home, and in your community. God is ready to release His heart through you, and the world is waiting to hear His voice.

In conclusion, the world needs you to rise up as a prophetic voice. Step into the fullness of your calling, knowing that God has equipped you to carry His word to a world that is longing for truth, direction, and hope. You have been empowered to prophesy, and the Holy Spirit is ready to lead you as you speak His heart into the world.

Don't hold back—step out in faith, trust in God's timing, and release the prophetic words that will transform lives. Go now, empowered to prophesy. Let your life be a continual testimony of God's voice, His love, and His power to a world in need of His truth. The Kingdom of God is waiting for you to speak, and the time to prophesy is now.

ABOUT THE AUTHOR

Tom Cornell is the Senior Leader of SOZO Church in Washington state, founder of Walk in the Light International and SOZO Network. Tom is married to his beautiful wife Katy and lives in the Puget Sound area with her and their three kids. He has been in ministry pastoring and teaching the body of Christ since 2008.

He has a passion to see the body of Christ moving from people with an orphan mindset to that of sonship; equipping the body to do the work of Jesus resulting in seeing the Kingdom of God manifested here on earth.

www.ingramcontent.com/pod-product-compliance
Lightning Source LLC
Chambersburg PA
CBHW071229090426
42736CB00014B/3020